WILDFOWLING
PAST & PRESENT

AN ANTHOLOGY

EDITED
BY
TONY READ

British Library Cataloguing-in-Publication Data
A catalogue record for this book is available from the
British Library

CONTENTS

SHOOTING WILDFOWL 1

SHOOTING CURLEWS - BY R.H.
FERRY. (1949) 9

SHORE SHOOTING - BY I. HUGHES
PARRY. (1947) 17

GEESE - BY C.T. DALGETY. (1937) 23

WILDFOWLER'S COMPANY - R.D.
HUMBER. (1947) 25

WILD DUCKS FOR SPORT - 1912 (ANON) 30

DUCK - BY E. PARKER (1918) 43

SHOOTING GEESE FROM PITS AND
TWO SHOTS AT BERNACLE GEESE - BY C.V.A.
PEEL. (1901) 56

MORNING FLIGHT - BY D. WALKER 64

SOME OLD METHODS OF
WILDFOWLING - BY W.A. DUTT (1906) 67

A PUNT GUN SHOT AT WILD
SWANS - BY J.E. HARTING (1883) 83

CHANCE OF A LIFETIME -
BY "SEPTEMBER RED" 96

IN QUEST OF THE PINK - FOOTED
GOOSE - BY JOHN HODGSON 1947 102

FOURTEEN RULES FOR PUNT-GUNNERS - BY. SIR
RALPH PAYNE-GALLWEY. (1887) 109

AN EARLY WIGEON FLIGHT - BY "SINBAD" 116

STANCHIONGUN BARRELS AND THEIR
MAKERS - BY CAPTAIN LACY (1842) 122

SOME FORGOTTEN EDIBLE BIRDS - BY H.A.
BRYDEN (1904) 130

GREY GOOSE SHOOTING AFLOAT - BY
STANLEY DUNCAN 139

GEESE IN THE GREAT FROST OF '47 - BY
J. WENTWORTH DAY 145

THE MAGIC OF GOOSE SHOOTING - BY
G.K. YEATES 159

WILDFOWL SHOOTING FROM "TUBS." - BY
MAJOR ARTHUR HOOD (1909) 165

A SOLWAY FOWLER - BY E. BLEZARD 178

FALKLAND ISLAND GEESE - BY 'KELPER' 183

IT COULD HAPPEN TO YOU - BY BILL
POWELL 188

FIRST MORNING FLIGHT - BY BILL POWELL 195

FIRST RIGHT AND LEFT - BY C.T.
HODGKINSON 204

A WILDFOWLER'S LUCK - BY C. RICHARDS 211

CRIPPLE STOPPING - BY CAPTAIN
LACY (1842) 216

GLORIOUS MUD - BY. J. PEARCE 227

THE MUD TRAP - BY R. ARNOLD 232

DUCK SHOOTING FROM THE
AVON "GAZES" - BY R. HARGREAVES (1903) 239

SOME GOOSE TALK - BY J. JONES 249

WILD FOWL SHOOTING AT HOLY ISLAND
- BY SIR RALPH PAYNE-GALLWEY (1909)............. 257

A NIGHT OF WILD FOWLINGIN THE NORTH
KENT MARSHES - BY W. HALLIDAY (1909) 260

THOUGHTS ON FLIGHTING - BY
B. ST GEORGE.. 268

WILDFOWLING AFLOAT - BY WALTER H.
POPE (1903)... 276

THE SPORTING COOT - BY A. JOHNSON........... 297

A SNIPE CENTURY - BY "CONRAD" 305

THIS WILDFOWLING FEVER - BY
COOMBE RICHARDS.. 311

Shooting Wildfowl

Wildfowl hunting or shooting is the practice of hunting ducks, geese, quail or other wildfowl for food and sport. In many western countries, commercial wildfowl hunting is prohibited, and sub-genres such as duck hunting have become sporting activities. Many types of ducks and geese share the same habitat, have overlapping or identical hunting seasons, and are hunted using the same methods. Thus, it is possible to take different species of wildfowl in the same outing – waterfowl are by far the most commonly hunted birds though. Waterfowl can be hunted in crop fields where they feed, or, more frequently, on or near bodies of water such as rivers, lakes, ponds, swamps, sloughs, or oceanic coastlines.

Wild wildfowl have been hunted for food, down and feathers worldwide, since prehistoric times. Ducks, geese, and swans appear in European cave paintings from the last Ice Age, and a mural in the Ancient Egyptian tomb of Khum-Hotpe (c. 1900 BC) shows a man in a hunting blind (a covering device for trackers) capturing swimming ducks in a trap. Wildfowl hunting proper - with shotguns - only began in the seventeenth century with the invention of the matchlock shotgun. Later flintlock shotguns and percussion cap guns have also been used, but in general shotguns have been loaded with black powder and led shots, through the muzzle, right up until the late nineteenth century. The history of shooting wildfowl is very much tied up with the development of the shotgun. It was the semi-automatic 12 ga. gun, developed by John Browning in the very early twentieth century which allowed hunters to shoot on a large, commercial scale. Once wildfowlers (primarily in America and Europe) had access to such guns, they could become much more proficient market hunters. They used a four-shell magazine (five including the one in the chamber) to rake rafts of ducks on the water or to shoot them at night in order to kill larger numbers of birds. Even during the great depression years, a brace of Canvasbacks could easily be sold, but legislation was gradually brought in to prevent such practices.

Early European settlers in America hunted the native birds with great zeal, as the supply of wildfowl, especially waterfowl on the coastal Atlantic regions seemed endless. During the fall migrations, the skies were filled with birds. Locations such as Chesapeake Bay, Delaware Bay and Barnaget Bay were hunted extensively. As more immigrants came to America in the late eighteenth and nineteenth centuries, the need for more food became greater. Market hunting started to take form, to supply the local population living along the Atlantic coast with fresh ducks and geese.

Men would go into wooden boats and go out into the bays hunting, sometimes with large shotguns – and they could bring back one or two barrels of ducks each day. Live ducks were used as decoys, as well as bait such as corn or grain to attract other wildfowl.

There are several items used by almost all wildfowl hunters: a shotgun, ammunition, a hunting blind, decoys, a boat (if needed), and various bird calls. The decoys are used to lure the birds within range, and the blind conceals the hunter. When a hunter or hunters sees the wildfowl, he or she begins calling with an appropriate bird-call. Once the birds are within range, the hunters rise from the blind and quickly shoot them before they are frightened off and out of shooting range. Duck or goose calls are often used to attract birds, but sometimes calls of other birds are simulated to convince the birds that there is no danger. Today, due to the ban on lead shots for hunting wildfowl over wetlands, many wildfowlers are switching to modern guns with stronger engineering to allow the use of non-toxic ammunition such as steel or tungsten based cartridges. The most popular bore is the 12-gauge. Only certain 'quarry' species of wildfowl may legally be shot in the UK, and are protected under the Wildlife and Countryside Act 1981. These are Mallard, Wigeon, Teal, Pochard, Shoveler, Pintail, Gadwall, Goldeneye, Tufted Duck, Canada Goose, White-fronted Goose, Greylag Goose and Pink-footed Goose. Other common quarry targets for the wildfowler include the Common Snipe.

An intimate knowledge of the quarry and its habitat is required by the successful wildfowler. Shooting will normally occur during the early morning and late afternoon 'flights', when the birds move to and from feeding and roosting sites. A long way from the market hunters of the eighteenth century, current wildfowlers do not search for a large bag of quarry; their many hours efforts can be well-rewarded by even a single bird. Wildfowling has come under threat in recent years through legislation though. Destruction of habitat also has played a large part in the decline of shooting areas, and recently in the UK 'right to roam' policies mean that wildfowlers' conservation areas are at risk. However, in most regions, good relationships exist between wildfowlers, conservationists, ramblers and other coastal area users. In America, the situation is rather different, due to the concerted efforts of J.N. Darling in the 1930s. He urged the government to pass the 'Migratory Bird Hunting Stamp Act' better known as the 'Federal Duck Stamp Act', which required hunters to purchase a special stamp, in addition to a regular hunting license, to hunt migratory waterfowl. This scheme has funded the purchase of 4.5 million acres of National Wildlife Refuge land since its inception in 1934. The Duck Stamp act has been described as 'one of

the most successful conservation programs ever devised.'
Thanks to such efforts, which maintain the natural habitats
of wildfowl, and especially of waterfowl, the sport is still
enjoyed by many, all over the world.

Wildfowling is the most romantic, exciting and challenging of all the field sports. All wildfowlers have a little poetry in their souls. The majority of fowlers are thoroughgoing individualists. Atypical wildfowler is a true hunter, bred and born–a lone wolf pitting his wits and knowledge against the wiles of some of the wariest and fastest birds on earth. Taking all this into account it is no surprise that wildfowling has fascinated a great many well known writers as well as inspiring many lesser known and even amateur writers to write with brilliance and passion about their sport. In this book I have attempted to select a number of gems and rarities of fowling literature from famous writers as well as including notes, articles and snippets from less well known, but nevertheless, enthusiastic scribes. This anthology will, I hope, help preserve some of the more obscure wildfowling tales for gunners of the future.

Several of the post war wildfowling stories include those of writers who contributed to now defunct sporting periodicals of that era. Their stories I consider masterpieces of the genre and have been included for the benefit of future generations. In some cases it has been impossible to communicate with them or their relatives, who may contact the publishers if they so wish.

THE OUTLOOK.

SHOOTING CURLEWS

By R.H. Ferry. (1949)

There is an old saying, "When a man has shot six herons, six wild geese and six curlews he may call himself a sportsman."

Herons and geese are certainly hard to get in range, but any stalkers skill is tested to the full by the caution of curlews, and the feeling of exultation is all the greater when one has been able to outwit such excessively wary creatures by superior strategy. Those who give up stalking curlews as a bad job and a waste of time do so chiefly because they go after them casually, in places where they are quite inaccessible of approach, unless by extreme caution and with more than a slice of good luck.

When small flocks of these curved-beaked and stilt-legged birds have been driven from their short feeding grounds on to adjacent moors and dunes by high tides, they have a habit of standing for long intervals to rest and digest their last meal. At such times the experienced leave them strictly alone, unless they have a great deal of time to spare. Every individual of these resting flocks is on the alert to observe the slightest sign of danger, and where rough ground might lend itself to an unobserved stalk, or, from the bird's point of view, favour a treacherous approach, all the greater caution is taken by them.

Where clumps of broom, rocks, or undulations obstruct a direct view, sentinel birds are posted on the higher mounds, and from these places of advantage they can easily see the most distant approach of danger. If their suspicions are in any way aroused they utter the shrill querulous whistle which is such a well-known characteristic of the species. Instantly the flocked birds raise their heads and look cautiously around, responding with answering cries of attention. If there is a second and yet louder warning cry the whole "herd" at once flies off with hysterical cries over the crest of the nearest hill or fold in the dunes. Occasionally an old and bold bird may come back over the gun as if to have a closer look at the enemy, when a shot is possible, but this only happens on a lucky day.

The feeding instinct of curlews is really remarkable, and in shore feeding birds, only equalled by herons. With correct timing, almost to the minute, they know when the shore has been laid bare sufficiently to allow of feeding, and arriving over the favourite site they wheel round and dip rather like plovers before landing. Some longshoremen take up a position in hiding and get in a few shots as the birds come over, but in my experience it is far better to refrain from firing till the curlews are well on the feed. This requires a good deal of patience, for before they feed the birds are just as cautious as ever–the horizon all round is well scanned and a good look round taken to see that the coast is clear, then they go to it in earnest with a fussy and intent precision. It is not always possible from a distance to see the movements of the flock clearly or to tell if the birds really have started the meal, and one may best gauge this by sound. On landing the flock breaks up into little groups and into ones and twos, keeping up a frequent interchange of communicating screams, which the stalker must do his best to interpret if he is to get within range.

With curlews there are always, under any circumstances, occasional wary cries from the ever nervy old birds, and here and there birds will start up in alarm, but with a little experience one is soon able to pick out "all clear" notes and twitterings of content and satisfaction. At he right psychological moment (a good deal depending on its exactness) it is possible to stalk up to a position well in among the fully occupied birds as they stand stretched out and scattered along the feeding grounds. Very strangely at this time the birds neglect to post "outlooks."

While I prefer to get the full satisfaction of a successful hunt operating lone handed, there is no doubt that two guns "working" the birds between them on prearranged signals, and with an unselfish technique, have a better chance of a big bag.

Like most birds that feed by feel rather than by sight curlews are active whenever the tide serves, by night or day. It is pleasant for a longshore sportsman and lover of wild birds to hear the weird wails of curlews on a rough night, with the murmur of waves or the roar of estuary water spilling over a sand bar, in the background.

When there is a moon there are few more fascinating sports than waiting for curlews under a tamarisk, bent over into natural hide by the prevailing gales. On the ebbing of the tide the mud flats gleam in the moonlight like a witch's mirror, and here and there the light catches one of the hundreds of runnels emptying themselves out into the estuary with chattering undertones. It is a ghostly scene, well befitting night feeding curlews. There seems always a moment or two of expectancy and lull just before all kinds of birds start pitching down. Many of the smaller birds–knots, plovers, dotterels, turnstones and "mud larks"–one cannot see, only the swish of wings on a still night, shrill pipings, cheeps and plaintive cries, make one aware of the presence of bird life. And then suddenly, from near at hand, a leading curlew gives an eerie whistle, and others communicate as they keep in touch in the uncertain moonlight.

It is advisable to let the leaders pass by and satisfy themselves that all is well. Before shooting one must turn towards the moon and wait until the silhouette of a curlew's beak and head shows etched against the round white target behind. Without a trained dog it becomes necessary to leave the hide to pick up the fallen birds, but in the moonlight, as with many other creatures, curlews loose a good deal of their natural caution, and liberties can be taken which could never be taken by daylight. Even so it is much better to remain at one stand than to move about in the hope of finding a better one. "Everything comes to him who waits" is a good slogan for curlew shooters on moonlight nights.

So many sportsmen who look upon teal, widgeon, and other "birds of a feather" as a gamey addition to the larder give away the curlews they shoot to their friends or enemies. In days gone by, however, as the old English rhyme shows, these birds were considered good to eat, even a delicacy:

"A curlew, be she white, be she black,
She carries twelve pence on her back."

Today this would be about five shillings.

The difference in colour refers to the darker hue of the old longer billed birds to that of the younger and lighter coloured individuals. A curlew is best hung by the beak till it will no longer support the weight of the bird. It must then be skinned, and backbone taken out, and an onion put inside the carcass the night before cooking. With the older birds I adopt the Highland custom of burying for a day or two—this takes any strong flavour out of the flesh.

But whether one shoots for the pot or for pleasure, there is always a subtle sensation of pleasure, mixed with vexation, as one plods heavy footed and listens to the birds that have outwitted the most careful efforts to stalk them. As soon as the back is turned the bubbling cry, half-wail, half-gurgle, comes over the air as contented curlews, in peace and safety, bore deep into the cool mud and feel the soft sea-slugs wriggling in their mandibles. The birds have been well named by those who live in solitary curlew frequented places, "Musical Wailers."

"FLIGHTING"

A whistle of wings in a storm-swept sky
At the meeting of day and night.
Shadowy forms are fleeting by
Clear to none but he fowler's eye.
Such is the evening flight.

Such is the sport that can try our skill;
Where the sluggard can have no part.
But the ear that is quick for the first warning thrill
And the hand that is steady may cope with them still.
The light is the fowler's heart.

F.A.Monckton 1913

"Mr. Meynell has had wonderful sport on his Laughton Estate (Lincolnshire) and his best season was in 1913 when, in three days, 1,086 Wild Fowl were shot: The largest bag was obtained on 6th October when five guns (Lord Lewisham, the Hon. R. Anson and Messrs. E. Meynell, G. Roadley and F. Meynell) killed 74 Mallard, 398 Teal, 15 Wigeon, 5 Shoveller and 1 Pochard = 493. On 3rd November five guns killed 89 Mallard, 236 Teal, 9 Wigeon and 21 Shoveller = 355, and on 8th December six guns killed 65 Mallard, 167 Teal, 1

Wigeon, 3 Shoveller, 1 Sheld Duck and 1 Pintail = 238. The great majority of these ducks were killed in the early morning flight."

SHORE SHOOTING

By I. Hughes Parry. (1947)

To men of a certain mentality, shore-shooting makes an almost overpowering appeal. Many men, really keen on this sport, would far prefer the couple of hours or less, morning or evening flight, spent in solitude and in the wilder weather the better, than a really good day's partridge driving or pheasant shooting in good company and under perfect surroundings, and it is to these men that the following lines are penned. I hope that some of the hints may be of value to them.

Perhaps the most important of all is to first find out your pet spot. It may be on the Island of Anglesey, or on the wild Carmarthen coast; in Devon or Cornwall, or on the Yorkshire coast. I know pet places on all these, and there are hundreds of others scattered around our coasts where with average luck one can fire from six to a dozen and a-half cartridges at almost every kind of bird from the lordly goose to the fast-flying redshank during both the morning and evening flight.

Naturally, with the present-day use of cars, local gunners are loath, until they become your friends, to give away favourite spots. A keen eye and a knowledge, especially of tide, will soon help one to find a likely place, always remembering that a tidal estuary, the larger the better, with a marsh or swamp at the head of it, makes the most likely place to find a good flighting spot.

What most shore gunners seem to lack to a great extent is imagination. Good camouflage is essential, and if one has a big peaked hat and waterproof long and loose, so coloured as to blend absolutely with the surroundings, and one stands or sits perfectly quiet, it is simply wonderful how little notice flighting birds especially will take of what they think is doubtless just a jutting rock or else an extra high bunch of rushes.

Last autumn I saw a man standing in a seven acre field of barley. He had on one of the old fashioned coats with a hood joined to it. This turned up over his head really made him look like a letter A without the centre stroke. On this someone had sewn a few stalks of barley, heads all more or less pointing up. It looked roughly done, but it did the trick, and with his gun held down between the lower opening of his overcoat, and about seven or eight well set up decoy pigeon around him, his bag from 3.30 p.m. until 8 or 9 p.m. came to 27 pigeon out of 35 shots. Some of these were shot sitting on surrounding stooks, say, roughly, 50/50 flying. The point is that at times pigeon nearly lit on the top of his head, and it certainly beat any blind I have ever seen.

Personally I have stood on the edge of a sea marsh in Anglesey with a painted mackintosh and a long pointed hood, where the rushes were not more than one foot high, and time and time again had curlew–can one find a shyer bird? I wonder if they have ever been shot at anywhere around–light within a dozen yards. Don't believe a curlew can't see behind him, even when feeding, and one's gun must be absolutely free to come up and no time wasted in taking aim. Shore-shooting in most cases is pure snap shooting, not as in usual shooting where one sees a bird coming and until he is in range he does not see you; but because you see the bird. But he does not see you *until you move.*

It is a wonderful test of nerve to have a dozen mallard or widgeon floating in on the tide and remain absolutely motionless until they are well within range. Decoys and calls can always be of use, each in its own place. But when all is said and done, flighting is really the highlight of shore-shooting.

Remember, the wilder the weather the better sport, and that one cannot be too early at one's stand and cannot stay too late. Many a good heavy mallard has met his death when really only just a shadow has been discernible against the very last ray of the long since set sun. Weather, of course, plays its most important allotted place in all flighting, as only a few degrees difference in wind will alter the regular flight of birds some 100 to 200 yards and when it is really fine and still one must be almost directly under the oncoming birds, and even then they are often out of shot.

A real good sea storm with frost is the prayer of many a gunner, who then, rigged out in his white cloak and white hood reaching from the point down on almost the same angle till clear below the shoulders, can stand even in the open and little or no attention will be paid to him, provided, as I said before, he stands motionless. Whether to have a dog with you or not is a very mooted point. But the scales are weighted, in my opinion, in favour if–and it is a big "if"–your dog knows the game and will lie quietly where you tell him to do so. Even, as I have often done, going as far as carrying a groundsheet and stretched it out on the bare sand and told him to lie under it, just allowing him enough space to keep his eye on you standing motionless perhaps some 20 yards away. Certainly when it gets really dusk, and the only way that one knows that a bird has fallen is by the thump on the ground or the splash of the water, then a dog is an absolute necessity.

It is a curious fact how curlew, godwit and many other shore birds will often swing in over a well-hidden gun when they see what they think is a lone dog wandering along, and if you both thoroughly understand each other often a good close shot can be obtained by letting the dog wander off a bit and work his way back slowly. For this type of work a crossbred Irish Water Spaniel-Labrador seems about the best. They are tough, hardy, and one can't tire them out. If you have a car and a long run back, always carry an old heavy 2-cwt. Seamless sack. Put him in and tie it round his neck and he will never catch cold, however wet and dirty he may be. They love it, too.

Guns and cartridges come next. Personally, a good 12 or 16 bore seems to me preferable to a heavier bore; but one must have different coloured cases for different sizes of shot. It is not hard to get cartridges without the shot in them from any good gunmaker, and one can then load with No. 2 or 4 or 6 shot to suit oneself. The highest shot I ever saw killed was in a morning flight in Anglesey by a lady with a 16-bore (MacNaughton, Edinburgh, gunmaker), with 7/8 oz. No. 4 shot, and I had let him, a cock mallard, pass right over me, thinking he was clean out of shot. She was sitting about 70 yards nearer the sea, under a sea wall, and he fell stone dead within ten yards of her, exactly as if he had flown against a pane of glass. On talking over it afterwards she said, "I did not think you had seen it, or else you were leaving it for me." But it certainly was right up in the clouds, and a big mallard always looks closer than it really is, whilst a high snipe, for instance, always looks far further away.

GEESE

By C.T. Dalgety. (1937)

The call notes of all four of the common grey geese overlap each other. The deeper notes of the pinkfoot are almost the same as the higher notes of the greylag. The higher notes of the pinkfoot are the same as the deeper notes of the whitefront. Neither pinkfoot nor whitefront can make so deep a note as that of the greylag. Neither greylag nor pinkfoot can make so high a note as that of the whitefront. The bean goose is a very silent bird. Its cries are half-way between those of the greylag and the pinkfoot. It has one, unmistakable note which is very much more gruff and hoarse than that of any other goose.

The calling of grey geese is usually termed "honking." Strong powers of imagination are needed to hear a grey goose say "Honk." Nearly always, the cry of the grey goose is monosyllabic. But even our own black geese do not say "Honk." The brent says "Crank" and rolls the "r", while the bernacle says "Yi." The Canada goose does make a noise like "Honk", and perhaps that is the cause of all the "honking"

23

in the wildfowl books. The actual calls of our grey geese are much more like: "Ga-ga," "Ngu-ngu," "Ya-ya," "Wa-wa."

For some years certain periodicals have been constantly publishing lists of "correct" names whereby to designate flocks of different birds and beasts. All these lists give the definition of "skein" as a flock of geese in flight and a "gaggle" as a flock of geese on the ground. Anyone with the barest knowledge of geese could not call a disorderly flying mob a "skein." A "skein" is obviously the correct word for designating the aggregation of wedges, while no better word than "gaggle" could be found or invented to describe the loudly calling, flying flock which has no ordered formation. Personally I prefer to go even further and talk of a "wedge", meaning a single wedge or V, a "skein" meaning a more complicated figure consisting of more than one wedge, a "gaggle" meaning a disordered mob, and a "flock" when the birds are on the ground.

WILDFOWLER'S COMPANY

R.D. Humber. (1947)

I am no hand with a gun. I lost a leg at the age of eleven as the result of a fall when following my first otter hunt, and blood poisoning set in. Being "winged" thus early in life and having an avid interest in wild life, I developed quite a capacity for making my other members work overtime. The rooks cawed happily in the old rookery when they thought their chief egg robbing enemy had been defeated, but I "capped" them next spring time by reaching some of the nests, despite the missing limb.

However, one cannot cope with the correct swinging of a gun on crutches, so my duck shooting consists of hiding in the reeds and rushes by inland pond and saltings pool sitting on a milk stool. A poor thing, but my own device, and the occasional bag of a widgeon, teal or mallard means as much to me as the royal stag to the deerstalker. What I have missed in personal prowess with a gun I have made up in enjoyment by accompanying local fowling friends on various expeditions.

A quest after greylags on a beautiful November evening was a memorable occasion. I had arranged in "The Duck Inn" to take a friend in my sidecar to the far side of the estuary. Roger was waiting beside the bay road below the village on the hill, a 12 bore resting on his shoulder when I drew up on the motorcycle. His lean weather tanned face grinned a greeting and he pointed his hand towards the west and said, "They're going in to feed on the stubbles." I gazed towards the fiery golden sky and watched a few small vee-shaped skeins of geese drift high over the bay and dip slowly down to the big reclaimed marsh on the far side. "Several hundred geese have flown in since I came down here," he added.

Roger stepped into the sidecar and the powerful bike hurried us round the bay road, with the keen, frosty air flaying our faces. We left the bike at the end of the rough, sandy lane, and walked over the long grass-banked sea wall. It is the task of the farmers who rent the three isolated moss farms to maintain the four miles of sea wall in good condition.

Rabbits continually undermine the banking and the high tides creep stealthily up, licking hungrily at the barrier which guards the land won from the sea. Life is no "golden glory" for these moss farmers. Sometimes a high autumn or spring tide breaches the wall and ravages the reclaimed acres, leaving behind a trail of drowned sheep and destroyed crops. Behind the sea wall we could hear the greylags feeding on the hundred acres of oats stubble, muttering together like domestic geese of the farmyard. At twilight they would rise off the stubbles and fly over the sea wall on their way to their nightly roost on the sandbanks in the middle of the bay.

Two other figures walked towards us from the far end of the sea wall. When they came nearer we recognised them as Roger's brother Will, and Tom, his wooden-legged fisherman friend. They had rowed across the bay in Tom's boat. Will was armed with a wicked looking 4-bore and Tom carried a long single barrel bolt action "gas-pipe," very similar to my own gun. Possibly they were both made by the same blacksmith; certainly no self respecting gunmaker would have owned them.

After a chat we took up our positions behind the sea wall; I stood next to Roger on the landward side. The sky had changed to flaming red and the sun was westering over the bracken clad hills behind the marsh. The estuary was clamorous with bird voices and the dusk seemed alive with whistling wings as mallard, widgeon and teal passed overhead. The hoarse sounding "gurr-gurr" of the female widgeon contrasted strangely with the lovely "wheeo" of the drakes. Curlew and oyster catcher mingled their clear, thrilling cries in the evening chorus. Across the bay a railway engine hooted and clanked out of the estuary station and a bus droned along the bay road. A myriad house lights gleamed on the far hillside as the seaside village lit up for the night.

We seemed to be in another world far remote from the human bustlings over the bay. Roger suddenly hissed excitedly, "They'll be off any minute now." The gaggling of the geese rose to a higher pitch, like the surging waves on a rocky coast. Then a hush came and I strained my eyes in the dying glow of the sky above the dark marsh. In a moment the sky seemed to be full of the great birds flying low in straggling formation. Tom fired first, and his hoarse excited voice claimed that he had downed one. I learned later that Tom had a habit of claiming any bird which fell after he had fired, whether the bird dropped close at hand or in the next parish!

I dropped my crutches and fired at the first of three geese which looked no higher than a couple of telegraph poles. They never even swerved and gaggled derisively as they sailed majestically over the bay. The 4-bore boomed and Roger's gun cracked twice. A goose swayed in the sky and hurtled to the sands with a dull crump. Several more satisfying bumps sounded along the beach and then in a lull during the shooting I heard Tom swearing vigorously at the far end of the line. It transpired that after he had fired his first shot the three inch cartridge jammed in the breech. Tom's language would have melted any ordinary gun, but penknife, teeth and curses failed to budge that empty case.

Several more flights braved the barrage and then we slithered about in the sandbanks and oozy gutters to collect the slain. Roger gathered three and the other two gunners picked up four geese, of which Tom claimed two. Roger and I walked back to the motor-cycle. Though I had failed to bring a feather down I had enjoyed every minute of it. Back in the warmth of the cheery inn parlour Roger laughed as he raised a pint to his mouth. He looked at me and said, "Tom did well to bring down two geese with one shot."

WILD DUCKS FOR SPORT

1912 (Anon)

There is, perhaps, no British sporting bird which has suffered more severely in comparatively modern times than the wild duck. Little by little it has been driven from its favourite haunts as the marshy parts of the country have been drained and erstwhile waste districts have been brought under cultivation or "developed" into residential neighbourhoods. The wild duck in its natural state is the shiest and most retiring of birds, and even though its actual nesting place may remain for a long time untouched, the wild duck will begin to fight shy of it as the surrounding country becomes gradually transformed by the busy workings of mankind. Almost every one of us can remember some place or other where twenty years ago, or even less, the nest of the wild duck was by no means a rarity, but where nowadays such a thing is seldom or never seen and except in a few specially secluded or protected districts, a similar state of things has come about in almost every county in the kingdom.

How extraordinarily plentiful wild fowl of many kinds must have been in days gone by we can easily discover if we care to turn to the records of the past. Before the days of the decoy, "duck-driving" was a favourite summer occupation of the populace in the fen districts, and so numerous were the fowl that, Daniel assures us, no fewer than 3,000 mallards were taken on one occasion in the course of a single drive in the fens about Spalding, in Lincolnshire. Willoughby tells us that sometimes as many as four hundred boats took part in these huge drives of wildfowl, and that he knew of as many as 4,000 birds being taken in a day at Deeping Fen. Again, Gough, in his edition of Camden, mentions that in or about the year 1720, 3,000 ducks were to his knowledge driven into a single net in one operation.

These summer duck drives were, of course, organized at a time of the year when the old birds were in the moulting stage so that they could fly but little, if at all, while the young ones, not being fully fledged, were also easily manoeuvred into the nets. The latter were V-shaped, and placed at the end of a lake, or pond, into which the fowl had first been driven from the surrounding marshes. There is an old print still in existence which shows how this duck-driving was conducted in mediaeval times, and it can readily be imagined that in spite of the enormous number of fowl bred in the country every year, these wholesale methods of slaughter eventually begin to leave their mark upon the wildfowl population of the country. Of course, their was no pretension of sport in the business- the whole thing was engineered simply with a view to profit, the flesh of the wild duck and other water-fowl being of considerable value in the market.

But at last it was seen that if such methods of wildfowl destruction were allowed to continue without some limit being imposed as to season, there would soon be very few fowl left in the country, and a most valuable source of food supply would be cut off. Accordingly in the year 1534, an Act was framed to prohibit the taking of wildfowl in this manner during the summer months. The Act remained in force for some years, but at length appears to have been repealed, since mention is made in later times of duck-driving in the summer still being practiced. In the fourth year of Edward VI.'s reign (1551) a petition against the Act was, in fact, presented to the King, in the following quaint terms:- "Whereas in the twenty-fifth year of the reign of your Majestie's father of most famous memory, King Henry the Eighth, an Act was made containing two branches, whereof the one was against the taking of wild fowl between May 31 and August 31, with any nets or engines upon a pain limited therefore as in the second statute more largely doth appear: and forasmuch as the occasion of the second branch appeareth sithen to have arisen, but on a private case, and that no manner of common commodity is sithen perceived to have grown of the same, being notably by daily experience, found and known, that there is at this present less plenty of fowl brought into the markets than there was before the making of the said Act, which is taken to come of the punishment of God, whose benefit was thereby taken away from the poor people that were wont to live by their skill in taking of the said fowl, wherebye they were wont at that time to sustain themselves with their poor households, to the great saving of other kinds of victual, of which they are now destitute, to their great and extreme impoverishing." So, as it appears, the embargo on duck-driving was removed, though it was at the same time provided that no person should take or destroy the eggs of any wildfowl under heavy penalty.

It is not quite clear, however, that duck-driving was ever illegal on private waters. At any rate, although at a later date the original prohibition seems to have been revived, there are frequent references to the taking of fowl in nets in such places during the summer in the seventeenth and early eighteenth centuries. As time went on, however, it came to be generally recognised that duck-driving was a foolish proceeding–perhaps the suicidal policy of such a practice became self-evident as the takes became smaller and smaller, as they must have done. And then when the art of duck-decoying in winter was introduced from the Continent, the advantages of the latter method over the original system of fowling must speedily have been realized.

There are numerous records of the success which attended the establishment of decoy-ponds in various parts of the country, and one need only mention one or two of them to prove that with the adoption of more sensible methods of taking wild fowl, the birds once more became numerous in all suitable districts. But no doubt a large proportion of the fowl taken in the decoys during the winter season consisted of birds that had been bred outside the country—we know, indeed, that many kinds of fowl so taken were of a kind that have never bred, or only in very small numbers, on British soil.

In these days it is almost impossible to believe that so many fowl could have been met with in the fens, but the records that have been handed down to us appear to be authentic, and surprising as the figures given may be, we have no good reason to doubt their possibility. Pennant records that no fewer than 31,000 ducks were taken in a single season among the ten decoys situated in the neighbourhood of Wainfleet, in Lincolnshire, while even in the last century the average yearly take of one decoy in the same county—that of Ashby—amounted to nearly three thousand fowl, over a period of thirty four seasons (1834-1868).

Today, however, the duck-decoy has had its day, partly because of the increasing scarcity of fowl, owing to the natural causes already referred to, and partly because the claims of shooting as the most sporting of all methods of wildfowling have come to be properly recognized. It may be said, in fact, that as the old decoys have one by one ceased to exist, and as the popularity of shooting has increased, quite a new era in the history of wildfowling has sprung up. And this new order of things, which is simply the evolution of the law of supply and demand, tends to do as much as is now possible under such changed conditions to set the wild duck on a better footing than it has enjoyed at least within the memory of anyone now living.

As gunners became more numerous year by year, and as other adverse influences made themselves more severely felt, the supply of wild fowl soon proved itself quite unequal to the demands made upon it, and it became abundantly evident that if anything worthy of the name of good sport was to be had, something would have to be done by way of giving the mallard a helping hand. Naturally, the idea of artificial preservation occurred to someone, and the experiment of raising wild ducks by hand, much in the same manner as pheasants, was tried. And with equal success. It was found that if the birds were properly looked after there were few losses, and that if the feeding were not overdone, and the eggs procured came from a good flying strain, the very best of sport might be obtained from birds brought up from start to finish under artificial conditions.

Today, indeed, it may be said that there are scores of estates all up and down the country upon which the annual rearing of a quantity of wild duck for shooting is considered just as much part and parcel of the gamekeeper's business as the bringing up of pheasants for covert shooting; and at the same time the game farmer has turned his attention to a branch of the business which, judging by the extent to which it has been developed in the last two or three years, appears to be eminently profitable.

It was only to be expected, however, that there would be some sort of an outcry against the introduction of artificial methods into a branch of sport whose surroundings from time immemorial had been so entirely natural as those associated with the wild duck. The very name of the bird seemed to be an argument against any kind of interference with its natural habits, and all the same arguments that were brought forward to the detriment and ridicule of pheasant rearing were again levelled at the practice of bringing up wild ducks under the keeper's care.

The idea of a "tame" wild duck seemed to tickle the critics beyond endurance. The hand reared mallard has, however, long ago managed to live down the ridicule that was hurled against it, and if there still remains anyone who is of the opinion that the bird is incapable of providing just as good diversion as any purely wild wild duck that was ever hatched, let him go and look on at the shooting that takes place annually at such places as Lord Rothschild's at Tring, or at Wadhurst Park, in Sussex. Any sceptic would soon be convinced once he had had a half hour's view of the duck shooting as conducted at either of these places. There is, indeed, in the opinion of many, no bird harder to bring down, once it is well on the wing, than a wild duck, and it makes not the slightest difference whether the bird is truly wild or hand reared, so long as the shooting is properly conducted. But on that point the ducks generally manage to look after themselves pretty well. Once the shooting begins it is not many unfair chances that are offered, and the man who picks only the very easiest of the shots will not get much shooting.

A keeper, however, must know his business thoroughly if he is to get the best out of his hand reared wild duck. Though the birds are easy to rear, there are a great many points to be attended to, the neglect of any one of which may end in failure. An early start is very important, for although the wild duck matures quickly, it takes a long time to attain to its full power of flight, and it is a pity to shoot the birds until they are at the top of their form in every way.

The birds that provide the best sport are those that are hatched not later than the third week in April, but if they can be had earlier so much the better. Eggs can often be obtained quite early in March, for the wild duck is an early breeder, her nest being one of the first to be found in the marshes. It is usual to bring out the eggs under hens, but very good results have been obtained with incubators, and young wild ducks do better as a rule in foster mothers than the chicks of game birds. It is a mistake to suppose that water is necessary to the birds during the early part of their existence. It may seem unnatural to deprive them of it, but the fact remains that young wild duck are better as a rule without access to water than with it. For drinking, of course, they must have plenty.

So soon as they learn to fly wild ducks must have a pond or stream which they can regard as "home," for without water all the feeding and attention in the world will not keep the birds from straying. It is important, too, that the hours of feeding should be regular, for if the birds are disappointed a few times of their accustomed meal, they will begin to look about for food elsewhere, and it is quite possible that they may fall in with some other lot of ducks looked after by a keeper who is more regular in his methods.

A few pinioned birds are of great assistance towards keeping the main body of the ducks at home, and there are some keepers who find it an advantage to have two or three couple of the little white "call" ducks, which were often kept on the old decoy ponds. It is a bad plan, however, to have many of these, as they are of a restless and noisy nature, and their presence in too great a number disturbs that peace and quiet which is so essential to success. When a stream is available it is a good plan to feed the ducks in two or three particular places, and to ring the changes regularly from one the other. The plan has the effect of making the birds eager for their food, and it gives them good practice in flying from place to place, thereby making them strong on the wing at an early stage of their career.

When shooting time arrives the success of the proceedings will depend very largely on the skill of the keeper in placing his guns, and if no natural cover for the latter be available, screens will have to be erected. The position of the screens will depend upon the behaviour of the birds when flushed, and this can only be ascertained by experiment. There will be time enough before shooting begins to flush the birds a few times, and after that the screens may be put up in the places most likely to provide good shooting. They should not, of course, be so near the water that the guns may be tempted to fire before the birds are well up, though after the first shot or two, there will not be much to trouble about in that direction. Screens, by the way, are best made of double hurdles rather than of single ones, in order that the guns may be able to keep out of sight without having to change their position according to the direction in which the birds are coming.

It goes without saying that wild duck bred for shooting should not be harried too often, or they may forsake the place before half of them are bagged. Shooting may begin in September, and may go on every ten days or a fortnight until the bulk of the birds have been killed. In some places it will be necessary to shoot the birds sooner than in others for fear of loosing them, but when a few can be kept back to provide a stand or two by way of a little variety to a day's covert shooting, the value of such birds will be fully appreciated. When it has attained its full winter plumage, say, in late November or early December, your hand reared wild duck, 40 yards up, and coming at the rate of 40 or 50 miles an hour, is a bird that from the gunner's point of view, is bad to beat.

WILD DUCK SHOOTING WITH DECOYS.

DUCK

By E. Parker (1918)

A stretch of foreshore, uncovered by the tide, runs to a jutting headland and a misty horizon of sea. Levels of sand lie between ledges and ridges of rock. The sand slopes to the rim of the tide. There are broad plateaux of rock slippery with oarweed and bladderwrack, and opposite a gap in the cliff a rough roadway for carts and boats. For half a mile out the sea swings and sways, smooth with floating ice; ice crusts the foreshore pools, bent and shrunken as the outgoing tide has drunk each pool lower; the smell of ice is in the wind; from the south a gleam of sun lights the cliff, the seaweed, the sand.

It is the strip of shore on which I shot my first wild duck, and not even my first grouse survives in a more vivid setting. Still I see the flicker of white on his fast beating wings; still his neck points straight and long; still the sunlight shines on the green layer of the pool where he fell, the water sparkles on his throat, his orange feet splash the ice. To a boy of today, of course, a wild duck is a bird no rarer than a pheasant. But in those days, to one whose earliest shooting was inland, away from lakes and rivers, a mallard was bird dreamed about, a bird of the future, of distant waters to be walked by on heroic mornings. We carried him home; one of us was to skin and stuff him; later, he was to serve for a hunter's meal. But he was a bird of the sea shore, and not as a duck may be who has fed in the wheat fields. He had been nourished on a fishly diet, and the cook, though a woman of fortitude, abandoned him and opened her windows. Ask not of that evening.

To the same year belongs an afternoon as calm and sunny as that morning was icy and blown by Boreas. It was in Yorkshire, and that year all the late September days were sunny, or so I remember them. We had just come in from partridge shooting, as tired as boys should be, when news was brought such as should make the lame walk. Duck had come in; duck were there, on the pond, actually in the garden; there in very deed they swam, they were to be surrounded, they should hardly escape us who should surround them.

We were out at the first word; the pond lay some distance from the house; it was to be approached from east, west, north, south, at once, in silence, from behind heather, rhododendrons, fences, banks; we went by devious paths. Which way would those wary fowl leave the pond? How should we flush them, how deal with them when flushed? Only one way did each of us pray that they should fly, which was our way; yet was even that a prayer without doubts? Each, I am sure, foresaw them upspringing, six, eight, twenty of them, from the water, with splatterings and quackings; each imagined the necks outstretched, the wings beating, the twenty all coming one way, all within range-within range of him and none other; each thought of an uplifted gun-his gun-and triggers pulled twice; the twenty speeding on untouched, having flown over one gun's head-his head; each dwelt after that upon the thought of the moments to follow, the questions, the remarks of others, the evening, misery.

But misery came not my way; neither misery nor ducks. We stood by the sides of the pond; there was silence, then a nervous chattering among the reeds; their heads were up, we knew, and the next second they were up themselves, with a prodigious clattering of pond water. They chose all one way, over the head of him who had organised the surrounding of them; one fell and not two; so the sun went down that day on a tempered joy.

When I think of wild duck, it is not first of flighting, or of duck at a great height, or of the best form of shooting; it is of these earlier birds first, and of others like them. I think of south country trout streams, of Hampshire water meadows, the mauve of a grayling, dabchick like live bubbles, a mallard and his mate winging up from the bend of the stream. I think of Highland lochs and duck rising from rushes at the earliest sight of the gun coming over the brae; of low ground between broken banks of heather, and tiny pools among sphagnum and sun-dew; of a burn that runs the length of a Forfarshire glen, and blackcock and duck in one wet spot year after year; of a Perthshire strath, of black-headed gulls turned grey, and duck dusky and undistinguished; of a snipe bog in Wales, a winding stream under high banks, mallard and golden-eye in the same bay. I think of midwinter, snow, a drake's most brilliant plumage, sunset, hissing logs in the hall. The schoolboy vision remains; the better shooting belongs to the later years, but in the clearest setting are the mallard and his mate, one after another, the easy shot for a boy, the luck hoped for, the trophy to bring home.

But flighting days are never far away from any thought of wild duck. One or two, indeed, are among the earliest memories; I am not sure whether I should put one of them first of all.

It was a winter morning; one of those mornings when a full moon is hidden by mist flying high, but with little wind, so that you walked in a world of cold and quiet as if it were lighted through a ceiling of white china. We left the road to cross fields dotted with dung heaps waiting for spreading; the soil was like iron, and the dung heaps might have been heaps of stone. Then came a stretch of frozen marsh, then a long line of shingle, and I think it was not till we had actually taken our chosen places by certain groins that we realised that the weather had changed and that our walk would be useless. The driving mist sank lower; we could hardly see a dozen yards.

Were there duck passing overhead? We knew there must be; there were the swish and whicker of pinions, the mist was blotted suddenly with forms that fled. Above us we could hear the honk-honk of geese; how low and close it sounded, and how baffling, white, empty was the mist! The minutes went by; the light grew, we knew the flight was over, and we had not fired a shot. Other mornings, other flighting hours have been spoiled by weather, and of other mists I have kept nothing but a sense of ill-luck and impotence; but that first morning, with its fields lighted by an unseen moon, its voices of unseen birds, the cold and vigour of it all, keeps still its spell.

It is a spell which belongs to a greater or less degree to all flighting, and for that reason I like the morning flighting best. With the evening, after a certain point, the chances lessen so rapidly that there is a sense of definite loss; it is a geometrical progression of vanishing opportunities of shooting, and the last term of the progression comes with the need to find and the possibility of losing what you have shot. Flighting in the morning does not add to its uncertainties that haunting sense of loss. The light grows, the mysterious distances clear into assured forms and presences, and you can see and retrieve. There come back to me mornings set long ago in the spacious idleness of Connemara; mornings when I used to stand an hour before dawn on a bridge between two loughs, and watch the slope of the hill, the current of the river, the distant islands growing out of the dark. The spell of cold twilight lay from the bridge to unseen fields beyond the shore; it was about the lough, the chasms of those dark mountains, the spray whipped across the bay, the birds appearing and vanishing.

I remember the first morning I stood on that bridge; the air was suddenly full of gulls, flying silently and jerkily as only gulls fly; yet I had seen no gulls before that morning. Duck were on the wing before it was light enough to see them; you heard pinions and they were gone. Duck swung into a grey sky: a couple, a single duck, a V-shaped flock, another flock, another couple; a skein of geese went by far out of range; you looked up the arm of the lough to the mountains, and it was broad morning.

There is a pleasure of surprise which duck more than any other bird bring into a day's shooting. Duck suddenly sweep into your view and are out of shot. Other birds spring surprises; snipe get up from a dry corner, woodcock come into a grouse drive, but duck swing out of distant skies unseen till they are close upon you, avoiding nothing, intent only upon flying as fast as possible from the place from which they come to the place to which they go. A bunch of widgeon, white and chestnut, flash down the foreshore. Teal are in the sky, wheeling dark and light, and you had not seen them till they wheeled. A mallard flounces over the trees, faster than you believe as you raise your gun. Wild duck, too, have a habit of surprising with numbers; numbers which escape. You can get no more than a right and left out of a big lot of duck, just as you can only get two or three out of a pack of grouse-unless they are strung out-but in an illogical way you are the more oppressed with failure with a big lot than with one or two. Many such surprises come the way of all of us.

Two such failures do I particularly recollect: twice, on successive days, within twenty-four hours, did I separately and deeply suffer. On the first day we had spied a flock of duck in a bay behind a string of islands at the head of a narrow arm of water. The idea was that one of us would row up outside the islands, and come down inside; the ducks then, we hoped, would fly within range of one of the islands where landing was easy and the rocks high. Therefore I landed upon that island, and he, that other who planned with me, rowed away. I had made out that he would take so long to get to the end of the string of islands, and so long to turn, and that the duck, if rightly guided, would pass over a certain central rib of rock where I should abide. There I so abode, and so, over that rib, did they pass. But it was before the boat was out of sight; before I had loaded my gun; it was while I measured the height of osmunda fern round me, and leisurely glanced above the sodden brown spikes of it; it was then that I heard a whicker of pinions, that I thrust cartridges into a breech with fingers too slow and too clumsy; it was then that thirty, fifty, sixty wild duck, flying at thirty, fifty, sixty miles an hour whistled, whirred, whizzed over my head, and were gone. Someone, something had disturbed them before he, that other, had rowed to his appointed place; and in five minutes more he, having seen all on the wing and all sweeping straightly over the chosen spot-he, I say, having seen and heard all, expectantly returned.

The morning of the next day was cloudless blue. We made a plan: Another arm of the lough, another boat-row, and another landing on an island. The boat was to be rowed as other boats had been rowed, trolling a line for pike; thus was an angler to beguile credulous fowl. It was to return not by deep water, but close by the reeds: the duck, it was in this way planned, would rise before the one boat and fly over the gunner landed from the other.

So they did fly; but they flew the very moment that they saw the first boat, so that they came over the gunner in the second boat before he had landed according to schedule; and he, in a vessel that rocked and swung, dealt with those duck and that opportunity as ill as he had dealt the day before. An hour later, it is true, he picked up on the shore of a neighbouring island a single mallard which the boatman readily recognised as the first he had shot at. But that boatman, it is certain, would have been equally willing to agree that the bird had been killed the day before yesterday or on some other occasion by any other person. Could it have been shot by Mr. O'Riordan, from the lodge the other side of the lough? "He did, sorr."

A mallard rising from the waters offers the walking gunner a sporting if not a very difficult shot. A teal is a different bird. When he gets up out of reeds and rushes he has few virtues; though he belongs, for all that, to the best of days and to mixed bags in the Lowlands, to windy afternoons in October, to the soaking mosses and grasses of snipe marshes in Wales. But the true measure of him is his pace and beauty in a bunch on the wing. In morning sunlight, in the grey of the evening: I do not know which I would rather choose.

There is a wild shore in a Mayo lough which I associate most with teal; a savage place in the dark or in a storm, for the bed of the lough is split into gullies, deep water between half-seen ridges of rock. You can work a boat in and out of the passes, looking for your depth a few yards ahead; but you must choose a calm day to go so far and to risk the rib of the boat. Teal fly the length of those ridges, up and down and forward and back, flashing in the sun like redshank; and it is with those mornings spent in the fern and willows of those narrow islets in my mind that I should endorse the choice of a writer in *Bailey's Magazine* of some years back, who decided that the most difficult shot was the second at a bunch of teal - the shot which follows that marvelous explosion of flying birds, up, down, outwards, inwards, sideways, all ways; the second shot which so seldom adds "left" to "right"; the best of the bunch.

But were those mornings better than the evenings? The evening I think of oftenest has no shooting in it. We have drifted under reeds and bulrushes on a lake without a ripple, and the grey sky is suddenly swept by teal. A bunch of teal swing over the pines and dip to the water, shoot across a bay and rise to the pines, swoop from the pines to the reeds, sweep up again, swing away again, vanish, slide back from an unguessed distance behind us, drop as though they had finally made up their minds to pass the night in a particular cove far from us, shoot up as though they would abide nowhere that night at all. It is the flight of a swift, the swoop of a hawk; it has the swing of manoeuvre in it and the caprice of a butterfly; in the quiet of dusk in October.

It may happen very seldom that we shoot at, much less kill, pheasants forty yards above the gun; but have we not most of us seen very high duck? Home reared duck often fly round and round the point from which they are flushed so plainly and patently out of shot that nobody troubles to lift a gun at them. But often, too, they are a little less than clean out of shot, and at these great heights they are killed, sometimes as obviously dead in the air as the most scientifically shot pheasant. But a little less than clean out of shot may mean nearer fifty than forty yards away from the gun; and if duck can be shot that way, why not pheasants? The opportunity with pheasants, no doubt comes too seldom. With duck, it may even come too often.

It is sporting shooting, of a kind, at its best. But even the best of it; ducks flying in threes and fives and V's from pond to lake; duck flushed from the same covert with pheasants–is even the best of it, with the touch of artificiality that there must be in the presence of gamekeepers, and the knowledge of the care and trouble needed by any sort of preservation–is even that worth so much as the scantiest of sport in untouched and open wild country? Out of all the memories of wild duck shooting in covert and by inland lakes and ponds, out of the very best of those days, with all their high duck and all their hundreds of cartridges, I do not know which I would pick to set beside the memory of a single hour of plain flighting, at dawn or dark, with its changes and chances; with the wind blowing through it, and the smell of the weed, and the duck coming in or going out to sea; an hour in which, I dare say, I shot nothing.

LYING OUT FOR GEESE ON THE HIGH SAND.

SHOOTING GEESE FROM PITS AND TWO SHOTS AT BERNACLE GEESE.

By C.V.A. Peel. (1901)

When the rain comes down in sheets and a gale of wind blows all day, as it frequently does in the Outer Hebrides, one is tempted to stay indoors in a cosy chair by the fire. But exciting sport awaits the the energetic sportsman who puts on his mackintosh and sea boots and goes out to brave the elements. On such a day geese leave the great stretches of sand, where they have remained in perfect security, and, flying across the dunes, seek the large open meadows and stubbles in search of the succulent grass roots and grain. On such open ground it is, of course, impossible to get near them. Their line of flight must have been noted a day or two beforehand. They must be intercepted before they reach the feeding grounds.

You cannot dig a pit and sit in it in any comfort on the low-lying flats, for as fast as you dig one it fills with water, and you may bail and bail, but you can never hope to keep it dry. No; you must repair at once to the sand hills near the sea, and there dig your hiding place.

Now, there is no creature more sharp sighted than a goose, so that a great deal of ingenuity must be brought into play in the construction of a pit in which to hide from so clever a bird. It is a mere waste of time to dig in the first spot you come to, jump in, and expect to kill a goose from it. The bird will see you or the pit nineteen times out of twenty. There are a great many things to be considered before one thinks of beginning to dig. The direction of the wind is most important and must be considered first. You have noted where the geese lie secure on the great sand stretch, and you have noted that yesterday, when the wind was blowing due south, the geese came, flock after flock, over an exact spot. So far, so good. But today the wind has a lot of west in it, so that the birds, when they fly up, will make straight for the same place at first; but it will be noted that they will gradually be driven out of their course by the strong wind, and although they appear to be turning their heads and battling with the gale, they will fail to make that spot, but drift over some eighty yards to the east of the noted place of yesterday.

In the same manner, should the wind have shifted round more to the east, then the birds will be driven more to the west. Having well considered the direction of the wind and made your calculations accordingly, the next thing to do is to choose a suitable place for your pit. Unless it is blowing a hurricane and pouring "cats and dogs", there is no particular hurry. The geese have had their early morning feed in all probability, and have flown back to the sand stretches, where they will lie squatting with their heads tucked up under their wings until one or two o'clock, when they will all return. The question now arises. In which spot will a pit show least?

And here one requires a good eye, for the pit and the sand thrown out of the pit must harmonize with the surrounding ground. Having fixed upon a mound or sand hill with, if possible, plenty of long star grass growing upon its top and sides, a pit must be dug near the top on the side farthest away from the geese. It must be dug deep enough to allow the sportsman, when seated, to see over, or rather, through, the grass on top of the mound. No sand must be thrown on the top of the mound; that side of the pit must remain perfectly natural and untouched. The semi-circular wall behind must on no account be as high as the natural front, or the birds will be bound to see it and swerve just before they come within shot.

A great quantity of star grass must now be dug up by the roots and planted all over the outside wall of the pit, and this, if neatly and cleverly done, will often render the hide extremely difficult to find should the sportsman leave it to retrieve a goose. There is no more amusing or exciting sport than shooting geese out of a well thought out, well made pit, and the wetter and more windy the day, the more geese there will be on the wing. I have seen small lots of geese coming so fast one after another that it has been impossible to load quickly enough to fire at them all.

In order to make more sure of the line of flight, four or five such pits should be dug some fifty yards or so apart, so that should the sportsman find that the first lot of geese went wide of him, he could at once run and hide in another pit, as geese almost invariably take the same line until the wind changes. One must make ample provision for cold and wet. Choose a high spot, and water will not collect at the bottom of your pit. A horse rug wrapped around one's feet is an excellent thing. A sweater, great-coat, and oilskin should be worn; but don't wear a black oilskin, as it shows up so clearly, and don't wear a sou'wester, as it prevents you from hearing the gaggling of the geese and gives you a headache, and, above all, don't go to sleep, but keep your eyes constantly scanning the direction whence you expect the great birds. A big gun is a necessity to kill geese at the height at which they fly; for although they come extremely low on many rough days, no amount of ingenuity can prevent their seeing you and rising when coming within shot. I have often nearly cried when using a 12 bore at geese.

It is very difficult to keep the sand and wet out of a gun on such a day. The rain runs down the barrel and carries under the fore end with it an enormous quantity of sand, which so blocks up the gun that should it be a top lever, it is impossible to open it. The water will also trickle down the inside of the barrel. Never shall I forget my anguish when, after waiting in a pit on such a day as I have described for eight mortal hours, a couple of grey lag geese flapped slowly over my head and *both* barrels missed fire! I now put a piece of paper over the muzzle of my gun, another piece at the top of the fore end, and tie a handkerchief round the locks.

There are many discomforts while sitting in a pit. Everything gets covered with sand. The difficulty is to keep it out of your eyes, as your handkerchief is full of it and your hands covered with it. The rain gets down your neck. To prevent this, wear a "dish-brimmed" cap and a woolen scarf. The best gun for this kind of shooting, and one least calculated to break down, would be a double 8-bore with hammerless action and an under lever opening. With such a gun I would sit for hours and endure the discomforts of sand and wet for the grand excitement of goose shooting on a "dirty" day. The far away gaggle puts one on the *qui vive*, and makes one strain one's eyes to the utmost to catch the first glimpse of the noble birds. Nearer and nearer they come, swerving to the right and left in the gale. Will they come within shot?

No; they will pass a hundred yards to my left. No; with an effort they force their way right over me. The excitement is intense as I raise the great gun to bear upon the birds. Bang, bang, and two fine birds with outstretched wings come slowly to earth, which they reach with loud thuds. I rush from my hiding place to secure them, and dragging them along by the neck, race back again to my hide just in time to see other lots approaching. And when the fun is over, and you walk home heavily laden with the grand birds, how pleased you are that you did not stay at home by the fire on that wild wet day.

✽✽✽✽✽✽✽✽✽✽✽✽✽✽✽✽✽✽✽✽✽✽✽✽✽✽✽✽✽

For days I had been trying to get near a huge gaggle of bernacle geese which flew on to the mainland from numerous islands, the grass on which was almost exhausted. Although I had stalked them by day, and waited patiently for them by night, I could never get within gunshot of the wily birds.

But at length the chance came one wild, wet day. On looking out of my bedroom window I beheld the rain coming down in sheets. The clouds showed no signs of breaking up. There was nothing else to be done; it was too miserable to stay indoors and watch the rain beating against the window panes. It was, however, an ideal day for geese, so, having donned thick boots and mackintosh, I sallied forth into the gale, accompanied by my brother and the keeper, the latter being very keen.

We had a long walk before us, but luckily the wind was at our backs, and blew us along. The tiny burns of yesterday had now been transformed into roaring torrents, and we crossed the old wooden bridge, under which rushed the yellow spate, with a shudder. At length we reached a low-lying stretch of sand hills, and we left the road to cross it. There were no rabbits out on such a day; the place seemed deserted. Nothing could be heard but the wild, weird scream of a curlew above the gale. We walked along in silence; it was too exhausting to shout at each other. In a mechanical way we walked straight across to a small green hill, along the top of which ran a stone wall. Up the green bank we marched, and sat down in comparitive shelter behind the wall.

From the top of this hill we got a fine view of the mainland, the sea, and the near islands. Out came three glasses for a spy. There was nothing on the green flat below us, but we soon discovered an enormous flock of bernacle geese, which literally covered a small island, which was seperated from us by a narrow channel. They were feeding greedily, their heads being turned up wind and towards us. It was a grand sight as they slowly marched like a huge army towards the sea. At length a little advance guard reached the edge of the grass, put up their necks, began to gaggle, and finally rose, and, flying low over the waves, crossed the narrow channel and settled again on the green flat below us. No sooner had they landed than another score reached the edge of the grass, and, coming across, joined the first lot. Then came a lot of eight, followed by several lots of from five to twenty or thirty, until not one remained upon the island. How we longed to have been down below with a noiseless powder for such a flight!

MORNING FLIGHT

By D. Walker

Cold and wet in a tidal creek when I might have been in
bed,

Seaboots fast in clammy glue, with the lights of the sea
ahead.

Freezing salt on frozen face, fingers stiff and numb,

Watching the racing breakers from whence the grey geese
come.

Grey as the sky before the dawn the mudflats merge the sky,

Lone as the drifter's barboned wreck this silent gunner, I.
Mixed with the music of the surf the distant dawning call.

Rousing the sleeping armies beyond the old sea wall.

Silver shot on the wavetops white the lazy dawn creeps on,

Drowning the flowing gale-swept tide the distant clarion:

Out of the growing brightness that dims the morning star,

At hedgetop height a thousand fly, two gunshot lengths too
far.

THE FOWLER AND HIS HOME.

SOME OLD METHODS OF WILDFOWLING

By W.A. Dutt (1906)

Apart from the working of duck decoys and the use of stake nets on the North Norfolk coast, wildfowling is rarely practiced in East Anglia now without the aid of weapons of percussion, in the shape of swivel and shoulder guns; but years ago, when marketable wildfowl, and especially the various species of duck, were far more plentiful than they are today, the professional fowlers, who must have been men well worth knowing, resorted to some curious means of wildfowl capture, which nowadays are seldom or never heard of.

Particularly was this the case in the Fen district, which, in the days before the drainage schemes were perfected, had an extraordinary abundance of resident water birds, and in autumn and winter was visited by immense flocks of migrant fowl. Indeed, John Fuller, when writing of the Lincolnshire Fens about the middle of the seventeenth century, seems to have found it hard to credit the stories that were told regarding the skill of the local fowlers, for he quaintly says:

"Lincolnshire may be termed the *Aviary* of England, for the *Wildfoule* therein; remarkable for their (1) *Plenty*, so that sometimes in the month of August, *three thousand Mallards*, with *Birds* of that *kind*, have been caught at one draught, so large and strong their *nets*, and the like must be the Readers belief; (2) *Variety*; no man (no, not Gesner himself) being able to give them their proper names, except one had gotten Adam's *Nomenclator* of Creatures; (3) *Deliciousness: Wildfoule* being more *dainty* and *digestible* than *Tame* of the same kind as spending their *grossie* humours with their activity and constant motion in flying."

But in those days large tracts of the fen country were in what Gough's Camden calls a "state of Nature," and the once famous East Fen was "a vast tract of morass, intermixed with numbers of lakes, from half a mile to two or three miles in circuit, communicating with each other by narrow reedy straits;" so there is nothing improbable in the statement as to the number of birds caught, and their abundance in the Fens. Indeed, the eccentric William Hall, who was born at Willow Booth, a small Lincolnshire Fen isle, in 1748, mentions the assertion of the old decoymen, that on a certain decoy pond, three acres in extent, the ducks were at times present in such numbers, that "it was apparently impossible for an egg to be dropped without hitting one," while at a mile distance the tumult of their rising from the water was like the sound of distant thunder.

Those were grand days for the Fen fowler, of whose origin and habits Hall gives us some idea in the curious lines he wrote, and which Mr. Southwell quotes in the *Transactions of the Norfolk and Norwich Naturalists' Society*:

"Born in a coy, and bred in a mill,
Taught water to grind, and Ducks for to kill;
Seeing Coots clapper claw, lying flat on their backs,
Standing upright to row, and crowning of jacks;
Laying spring nets for to catch Ruff and Reeve,
Stretched out in a boat with a shade to deceive;
Taking Geese, Ducks, and Coots, with nets upon stakes,
Riding in a calm day to catch moulted Drakes."

In crossing the Fen country by rail, one cannot help noticing the isolated situation of some of the farmsteads dotted here and there over the wide levels. In some cases the only road near them is the railroad, and even that is of little use to the dwellers on a farm, when their nearest station is eight or nine miles away. From one week's end to another the farmer and his family see no human faces save those of their labouring folk; they have to send for their letters to some main road cottage, which at times is barely accessible, owing to the state of the rough trackway leading to it from the farm; and if they receive a daily newspaper it is thrown from a train by a travelling bookstall boy, who flings it every morning from a carriage window at a small white flag stuck up beside the line.

These few facts help to suggest the conditions under which a certain number of the Fen-folk live today, and by imagining that the well drained levels around one of the isolated farmsteads are wastes of almost untraversable fen, and that the farmstead is a wildfowlers clay walled, sedge roofed hut, almost as damp as though it were roofless, we may gain some idea of the conditions under which many of the Fenmen lived as recently as a century and a half ago. At that time a typical Fen wildfowler and fisherman would have his home near one of the meres that were still undrained, and often this home, if not partaking of the nature of a lake dwelling, would be built on soil so swampy that the walls soon "settled" into angles markedly out of the perpendicular, and often were only kept from falling by wooden props or stays.

From his cottage door he would see, stretching away before him, an apparently limitless expanse of drained and undrained fen, dotted here and there with wooden windmills, low roofed farm buildings, and crazy cottages like his own; far away, beyond a labyrinth of dikes and fen banks, a fen isle only, with a few trees and houses on it, would break the monotony of the level horizon. From the mere he would hear the seasonable wildlife voices of reed birds or waterfowl; but often days would pass without his hearing a human voice save those of the members of his own family.

In summer, however, the conditions under which he lived would not be unpleasant, for then there would be no hardships to endure; but in autumn and winter, when the chill fog came rolling up from the mere and dikes, or the icy wind swept furiously across the shelterless wilderness of water and fen, he would often be compelled to lead a far from enviable life; for hours together, while at work with his fishing and bird nets, he would be exposed to the roughest of weather.

It is mid-October; the lush growths of the fens are withering, and boisterous winds have lately been making wild music among the reeds. For some days large and small flocks of fowl have been dropping in, among them being a number of pochards, or, as the Fenman calls them, dun-birds. For these, as they are a favourite dish with the Fen folk, the fowler has been lying in wait at nightfall, concealed in his boat among the reeds; and at daybreak, when they have been returning to the quiet spots where they rest during the day, he has been abroad and afloat again, taking toll of them as they collect together before taking wing.

As a result they have become shy and cautious, so he has decided to leave them undisturbed for a while and devote a day or two to plover netting on one of the wash lands bordering the river, this wash land having been partly flooded by letting the water on to it through a sluice. He starts for the wash early in the morning, rowing thither down a dike, and carrying with him his net and some live lapwings to serve as decoy birds.

On reaching the wash land he finds ten acres of it flooded to a depth of about eight inches, and on scanning the bordering lands, which are strewn with the stranded flotsam of a recent and more extensive flood, he soon detects some fair sized flocks of lapwings, some golden, plovers, and some wading birds feeding on the drying tracts and by the edge of the water. In the midst of the flooded portion is an artificial island made of sods of earth cut from a neighbouring dikeside: it is about twelve yards in length and two in breadth, and its surface is only a few inches above the water. To this island he wades, first with his net and its supporting poles, then with the wicker cage containing his decoy birds, and at once commences to fix the net in readiness for use.

This he does by spreading it out flat on the island, where it is kept extended by poles about four feet in length, each pole having at one end a leather joint, by which it is attached to a stake driven into the ground, and by means of which it can be worked to and fro. One edge of the net—that which is fastened to the lower edge of the poles—is then pegged down to the ground near the shore of the little island, and the fowler proceeds to make fast to the other end of the poles two lengths of rope which pass through pulleys made fast to the ground, and are then connected with a long line, by means of which he can at any moment pull the net over upon such birds as come within its range. This done, he takes the decoy birds from their cage and tethers them with string to small pegs driven into the ground just beyond the range of the net. The trap is now set, and the fowler wades back to the dike bank, behind which he conceals himself, holding in his hand meanwhile the end of the line that works the net.

For a while the decoy birds, rendered inactive by their cramped confinement in the cage, remain almost motionless; but the fowler has tethered them in such a way as to afford them a certain amount of liberty, and after a time they begin to explore the muddy margin of the island, seeking the worms which have been drowned by the flood. Presently the fowler imitates a lapwing's cry, and it is repeated by one of the decoys, with the result that an answer comes from a lapwing flock feeding on the unsubmerged portion of the washland. Again the fowler whistles a loud *pee-a-wee*, and continues to do so at frequent intervals, until a small party of lapwings detach themselves from the distant flock, and taking to wing, wheel erratically over the flood water.

They have seen the decoy birds, and, it may be, have deduced from their presence on the island that they have discovered there some succulent food; at any rate, after wheeling and tumbling for a while above them, they dip down and alight beside them. Then the hidden Fenman, who has been watching their movements from behind the bank, cautiously raises his head above it and gets a tight grip on the net rope. He sees the strangers join the decoys on the shore of the islet, and his patience is tested by their being content to remain for some time in the company of the tethered birds and beyond the range of the net; but presently some of them move nearer to the centre of the island, and others, having helped to clear off the drowned worms and grubs, follow their example.

With this movement the critical moment arrives. The fowler gives a quick steady pull at the rope, at the splash of which in the water the lapwings are alarmed, and at once rise from the ground; but before more than two or three of them are beyond the reach of the net, it comes sweeping over them and falls flat on the surface of the water, imprisoning them beneath it. Then the fowler springs to his feet, wades quickly towards the island, takes the captive birds one by one from beneath the net, and wrings their necks.

Before dusk descends upon the fens this method of plover netting has been several times repeated, the decoy birds having meanwhile been kept active by fresh food being thrown to them after each cast of the net. And should lapwings continue to be plentiful around the washland, the net may be worked for several days, until, perhaps, a sharp frost drives the birds from the lowlands. Nor are lapwings the only birds taken. Golden plovers, ruffs, knots, redshanks, and dunlins also fall victim to the luring whistle of the Fenman and the innocent abetting of his decoys.

A spell of frosty weather, however, drives most of the birds from the frozen fens, and those that remain–a few duck, teal, and wigeon–can only be netted in an elaborately constructed decoy. But our friend the Fen wildfowler is too poor to possess a decoy, and now that the lapwings and most of the waders have gone, he must rely on his punt and his shoulder and swivel guns to fill his bag and provide fowl for the carrier when he crosses the fens on his weekly round.

So long as there is open water on the mere he is afloat in his punt by moonlight and at dawn, creeping silently upon the feeding flocks. But night after night the frost grows keener, and at length, when he trudges down to the mere-side one morning about half an hour before dawn, he finds the ice so thick that he cannot get his punt afloat. The following night, and the next, the frost still holds, and then a day dawns which finds the fowler ready with another device for getting at the fowl.

He has made a stalking sledge. In some repects this contrivance resembles the creeping-carriage by means of which some wildfowlers approach fowl in the open, but instead of having wheels it is fitted with four marrow bones serving as runners. It consists of a long, low, raft-like framework, on which a swivel gun is mounted as in a gun punt; at the fore end a screen of reeds is held together by pliant withies; and behind this the fowler kneels on some dry sedge litter and pushes the sledge along on the ice by means of two iron-pointed sticks.

Day is just breaking when he slides his sledge on to a frozen inlet of the mere, and begins to work his way cautiously along the edge of a reed bed extending some distance from the shore. His progress is slow and silent, for he is careful to keep on smooth ice, and avoid dry and broken reed stalks which might crackle beneath the runners of the sledge, nor does he make a sound when he touches the ice with his pointed sticks. At the extremity of the reed shoal he pauses, and scans the frozen surface of the wide lagoon. Eastward there is a brightening of pallid light along the horizon, against which the distant reed tops and a canvas sailed windmill are gradually revealing clean cut outlines; westward, where an undrained jungle of fen sedge represents a former extension of the mere, the shadow of night still lurks among the thickets of sweet gale and the frost whitened blades of sedge.

In the dawn light the ice in the creeks is like dark glass through which the rotting water weeds are seen; but away from the shore, where wind rippled water has frozen around islets of reeds and rush, the ice has a white coating of rime. Hardly a breath of wind is now stirring—not enough to make the ice crystals tinkle among the sedge—nor for a while does a sound break the silence of the mere; but before a rosy flush has spread along the pallid streak of dawn light, an immense flock of starlings rises from the sedge fen, and the air is filled with the tumult of their wing beats as with that of a wind gust beating on a wood. But the flock, after sweeping upward and around as though it were caught in a great wind eddy, soon vanishes in the direction of the far distant ploughed lands, and then there is silence again until some bearded titmice awake and make fairy music in a rimy tangle of reeds near the fowler's sledge.

For half an hour or more the Fenman crouches in his sledge, breathing now and again on his fingers, which are growing numb with cold; but after the starlings have vanished and the titmice have taken flight to a neighbouring creek-side, the only birds he sees are three or four hooded crows which fly heavily over the mere. So presently he gets to work again with his pointed sticks, and slowly propels the sledge towards the nearest of the reed islets, round the edge of which he creeps until he gets a clear view of other islets lying beyond it. These he scans with the trained eye of an experienced fowler, and apparently is satisfied with what he sees, for he continues his slow progress over the ice until he reaches a clump of rushes, keeping his eyes meanwhile on an islet from which is heard at length the long drawn quacking of a mallard.

Even now, however, he is not within range of the fowl, and to get nearer to them he has to venture out on to an open expanse of ice, and rely on his screen of reeds to cover his approach. So he resumes his stealthy stalk until he is within seventy yards of the duck, which he can now see resting quietly on the shore of the islet; then he stops the sledge, lays down his sticks, and takes careful aim at the unsuspecting birds through an opening in his screen of reeds. The great swivel gun flashes and booms, the sledge is jerked backwards by the recoil, and the wildfowler, shoulder gun in hand, hastens over the ice towards his victims.

To take leave of the Fens and turn to the Essex marshes, we learn from Daniell's *Rural Sports* that years ago, when enormous numbers of pochards visited these marshes, they were taken by wildfowlers with the aid of a decoy called a flight pond and some curiously worked nets. These nets, which were fastened to poles from 28 to 30 feet long, were spread flat on the reeds beside the pond; but the bottom of each pole was weighted with a box full of stones in such a way that directly an iron pin was withdrawn, poles and nets rose upright in the air. Nets of this kind entirely surrounded the pond, and immediately within each was either a trench dug in the ground or a pen made of reeds about three feet high.

The fowler's method of working these was to conceal himself near them at the time when the pochards generally visited the pond, and wait until a good number of them were disporting themselves on the water. He would then, by a sudden noise, cause them to take flight, and as they, like other wildfowl, flew against the wind, he would immediately unpin the poles of the net over which they were passing. The net at once rose up and swept the birds into the pen or trench beneath it, from which they were unable to rise owing to their numbers and the shape and shortness of their wings.

No mention is made of the use of decoy birds in connection with this method of wildfowl capture; but at the present time,

79

when a similar method is resorted to in the taking of lapwing, both stuffed and live birds are used as decoys. As in the old days, the favourite spot for plover netting is a small island in the midst of a flooded marsh, and according to Mr. Nicholas Everitt, "the meshes of the nets are coloured the same as their probable surroundings, and the pattern used is the ordinary clap-net–known to all bird catchers–with the exception that one net only is used instead of two. Round the edge of the net stuffed peewits are set, and near the end nearest the fowler one or more live peewits are anchored down upon a small board, which, working on a pivot sunk into the ground, can be raised at the will of the string puller some little height into the air. The decoy birds are all placed head to wind, and the net is pegged down accordingly, so that when it is pulled over it will catch the birds as they are settling among the decoys. The poles of the net are about ten feet long, and the art of making a big haul is to allow the straggling part of the flock to pass and not to pull the net over until the thickest part of the flock can be reached."

This method of plover netting is practically the same as that practiced by the old time Fenmen, and here it may be mentioned that plovers are netted in the Fens today in much the same fashion as a hundred years ago. The wildfowler still constructs a long narrow island in the midst of a wash or a flooded marsh, but the decoy birds are usually tethered on separate islets about the size of mole hills. On the main island there is seldom a live decoy, but here are strewn a number of worms, which keep the first alighting plovers occupied until enough birds have settled beside them to make it worth the fowler's while to pull over the net. For his own accommodation he generally erects a small turf hut, around which a trench is dug to carry off the water in times of heavy rain. Outside this trench the excavated earth is heaped up in a kind of circular rampart, and the whole shelter somewhat resembles a model in miniature of a prehistoric camp. At the present time plover netting in the Fens is usually carried on near a windmill pump, by means of which the decoy marsh can always be kept flooded.

In the days when several of the Fenland meres were still undrained, large numbers of fowl were taken in nets known as tunnels, the particular method of taking them known as duck driving. These tunnels were decoy-like nets spread in a horseshoe form over creeks or dikes adjoining a mere, and they were generally used at the time when the ducks were moulting and before the young birds or "flappers" were able to fly. It was by this method that, as Fuller relates, "three thousand mallards, with birds of that kind," were taken at one draught in Lincolnshire; and it is also on record that in Deeping Fen 4000 ducks were so captured in one day, 13000 in three days, and, near Spalding, 2646 in two days.

For duck driving a day would be chosen when a considerable number of Fenmen could assemble and put out on to the mere in boats. They would then drive the fowl from the reeds and creeks on to the open water, where they would keep them together by splashing in the water with long sticks, and gradually get them to swim into the particular creek or dike which was arched over by the tunnel net. Once in the net, the birds were driven to the closed end of it, which was fashioned like the end of a decoy pipe; and there they would be taken out and killed.

This reprehensible method of wildfowl capture naturally resulted in a marked reduction of the numbers of ducks breeding on certain of the meres, and it is not surprising that in the reign of Queen Anne an Act was passed making it illegal to resort to this "pernicious practice," which was causing "great damage and decay of the breed of wildfowl." By this Act duck driving was prohibited between the 1st of July and the 1st of September, the penalty for breaking the law being a a fine of five shillings for each fowl taken, and the destruction of the nets.

A PUNT GUN SHOT AT WILD SWANS

By J.E. Harting (1883)

It was early in January, and the ground was covered with a mantle of snow to the depth of two or three inches. The harbour looked bleak, drear and deserted. Too shallow to be navigable except at high tide, and then only available for small craft, it was just the place of all others to attract wildfowl. Extensive marshes on either side, intersected by dykes, from which the dead reed tops showed through the glistening snow, gave promise of snipe and teal, to say nothing of a chance at larger fowl, and an occasional frozen out hare.

I had just come in after a long tramp over these marshes with four and a half couple of snipe, a teal, a golden-eye, and three golden plover in the bag, and was approaching the inn where I was staying, when I encountered a fisherman and wildfowler of my acquaintance, whose radiant face and unusually excited manner betokened that there was "something up." We had hardly approached within speaking distance when he hailed me with "Well sur, good news." "What," said I, "Some fowl in the harbour?" "Better than that, sur." "Geese. Eh? Black Geese?" "Better than that, sur." "What, you don't mean—" "Swans, sur, wild swans; five of 'em—two white 'uns and three grey 'uns, and they all be down in 'the Narrows' feeding, and there's no one seen 'em but me, and you'll have *just* a good chance at 'em, I believe!"

Here was a piece of news, then; something worth going after. Who wouldn't prick up his ears and finger his triggers at the mention of wild swans? But it was past five o'clock, dark, and the tide was out, and I had had nothing to eat all day. The last consideration would not have weighed heavily had there been any reasonable prospect of success by immediate action; but, on talking it over as we walked homewards, we agreed that the birds were not likely to be disturbed by anyone else, that they would be sure to remain all night in the harbour; and that, with so much snow on the banks and on the beach, I should stand a better chance of finding them by a morning light. It was, therefore, decided that I should be called early the next day, and that the punt should be in readiness with the long gun on board, and my large double under the fore peak in case of necessity.

Was it to be wondered at that I could hardly get to sleep that night with the prospect of what might be in store for me on the morrow? Tired as I was after a long day in the marsh, and eager to rise fresh and ready for perhaps another hard day in the punt, it was some time before I could compose my restless thoughts and forget for a while where I was. The crash of a handful of shingle against my window at early dawn came sooner than I expected. Hastily opening the window and looking out, I could barely distinguish surrounding objects and the indistinct form of the owner of the long gun, who informed me that the punt was alongside, and that everything was in readiness. As may be supposed, I was not long in making my appearance, and in finding my way almost in the dark to the harbour side. The punt lay alongside nice and clean, the long gun in its cover, and a rug thrown down for me to lie upon, everything just as it should be. As I shoved off into the darkness, a cheery "Good luck, sur," gave me encouragement to hope that our wishes might be realised, and that on my return the punt would hold another, though defunct, passenger.

THE BIG GUN.

THE PUNT FROM ABOVE.

As the spot where I expected to find the swans was considerably more than a mile away, and I knew all the channels pretty well, I decided first to get as warm as I could by exercise, and after working down to within a few hundred yards of what I knew to be the best feeding ground for swans, to lay up and wait for daylight. It was cold work, but a good thick Guernsey over a "cardigan" kept me as warm as circumstances would permit, while a nightshirt over all tended to prevent too great a contrast of colour between my moving figure and the surrounding white landscape.

As the punt glided onwards, and the land became lost to view, a strange sensation of loneliness came over me. The darkness, the stillness, the wide waste of water over which I was journeying, as it seemed vaguely, all contributed to make the situation a most exciting one. Occasionally the silence was broken by the weird cry of a curlew or a quack and a splash as some fowl dropped into the water ahead of me, and then all was still again.

Onward I went, making for a particular point a long way down on my right, where the sea wall ran out at a sharp angle into the harbour. From this point on a port tack, as a yachtsman would say, I could run for about five hundred yards and find myself in proximity, I hoped, to the birds. They could hardly have wandered very far from the spot where they had been seen overnight, and might possibly still be roosting on the beach.

Having reached the spot where I intended to lay up, I rolled myself up in my rug, and, lighting a pipe, lay head to wind and mused till daylight. As soon as I could see well, the telescope was pulled out, and I began to look about me. Several little bunches of wigeon were on the move, a heron or two, and three ducks, at a distance, which I could not at first make out, but which afterwards proved to be mergansers. The swans were nowhere to be seen!

I waited, moved on a little, and looked again. No, they were not on the water, they must be ashore somewhere; but *where* it was not easy to say, or rather to see, for the snow on the beach and on the harbour banks of course rendered it difficult to detect them against so white a background. There was nothing for it but to coast along within shot of the shore, and keep a sharp lookout ahead. This I proceeded to do, first using the glass to make sure the coast was clear, and then pushing along vigorously but quietly.

I had gone down the lower side of the harbour, round the bay in the southwest corner, and had proceeded for some distance to the eastward parallel with the beach, without seeing anything of the birds I was in search of. I began to feel uneasy, and to suspect that they must have been disturbed overnight and had left the harbour; but yet there was a chance of their being somewhere about, and there was still a good stretch of beach to be explored. Cautiously I paddled on for another two or three hundred yards, scanning the snow clad shingle on my right, until I could see just ahead of me the small uninhabited gravelly island at the mouth of the harbour, whereon I had made many a good shot at passing wildfowl.

On this island the tide casts up heaps of seaweed, and by banking some of this up with the aid of shingle, to keep it steady, a capital screen can be made from which one can command the channel, which flows on either side towards the sea. This island is a favourite resting place for the fowl at night, and it was not improbable that in the present instance the swans might have discovered and availed themselves of it. Such, indeed proved to be case, and it was not long before I could make out the forms of some of them on the side next the sea; they were busily engaged in turning over the heaps of seaweed that lay scattered about in all directions, and in the hard weather that then prevailed, found some little difficulty no doubt in procuring sufficient food.

They were in a favourable situation for getting at them, and the fact of their being so busily employed increased my chances of a shot. It was time now to get out the long gun and lie down to my work; and putting a couple of cartridges into the shoulder gun in case of need, I began anxiously to approach the island. As the punt drew nearer and nearer, I could make out the birds well without a glass. There were five, as I had been told, two old ones and three young ones, distinguishable by their greyer plumage. For some distance all went well. The birds were not alarmed, and I felt certain of a shot. As I crept within range, however, end on, I became aware that the tide, which was setting out through the channel, was causing the punt to drift, and that if I continued on my present course until within range I should find, on letting go the scull to take hold of the trigger, that I should be borne too much to the right, and the gun as laid, for it was not on a swivel, would be pointing quite away from the birds.

I was obliged, therefore, to keep the punt well above the island, so as to get my shot on drifting down past it. It was desperately cold–I could scarcely feel my fingers; but the excitement kept me alive, and it was now or never. Timing myself as well as I could, I got two birds in a line, and pulled. To my surprise and mortification, the cap snapped, and the gun missed fire. The swans left off feeding and looked up in my direction. Of course I kept as still as a mouse, but the punt continued to drift; and by the time the birds had become reassured and recommenced turning over the seaweed, I was some way out of my course, and had to get back.

It was a long time before I could feel and adjust a fresh cap, my fingers were so benumbed. At length this was accomplished, and again I was drawing near the island. This time by good luck I got the punt in a more favourable position, and, owing no doubt to its colour and that of the occupant, got pretty close–much closer in fact, than I expected. For the second time my finger was on the trigger; a moment of breathless excitement; a pull, and again a misfire! "Shiver my timbers!" as my man would say, this was too bad after all the trouble and hard work I had had to get the shot. But there was no time for reflection. The birds, alarmed by this second attempt, ran together with outstretched necks, and, spreading their wings, were just getting under way as I pulled out the old double, and, sitting up in the punt, let drive at the head of one of the white ones.

Just as I pulled the trigger he ducked his head preparatory to taking flight, and the charge floored a grey bird beyond him. Holding on him, however, with the left barrel, I had the satisfaction of seeing him come down with a broken wing; while the other three took to the air with loud cries, and were soon out of shot. They continued, however, to circle round for a long time, calling at intervals, and wondering no doubt why their companions did not join them. One, the grey one, was dead, being shot through the neck. The old white one was making off with a waddling gait as fast as his legs could carry him. It suddenly occurred to me that he was making for the channel on the other side of the island, and had he reached this and gone seaward I could not have followed him out of the harbour without a risk of being swamped.

Instead of pursuing him, therefore, from where I was, I pulled away, and went down channel with the tide, got round, and came up on the other side of the island, heading him back towards the centre of it, and then, running ashore and pulling the punt up, gave chase on foot. Although a stern chase, this time it was not a long one, for swans are not formed for rapid movement on the ground, and he was soon overhauled. But the difficulty was to know how to kill him. In the excitement of the moment, I had forgotten my gun, and, seizing the uninjured wing, which flapped away vigorously, I found myself the next moment sprawling on the shingle. My foot had slipped on the rolling surface, and down I came, swan and all. Up again, and still holding on; this time I had him by the neck; incautiously letting go the uninjured wing, with which I was soon severely buffeted. Never shall I forget that struggle! How we tumbled about on the beach, making the shingle fly in all directions, until, from being benumbed with cold, I almost perished with the exertion. He positively declined to have his neck broken, and a task indeed it was to break it.

But at length he succumbed, and as his lifeless form lay stretched before me on the beach, I was reminded of that scene so vividly painted by "Christopher North" in his description of the death of a wild swan upon a Highland loch: "to have shot such a creature–so large, so white, so high soaring, and on the winds of midnight wafted from so far–a creature that seemed not merely a stranger in that water, but belonging to some mysterious land, in another hemisphere, whose coast ships with frozen rigging have been known to visit, driving under bare poles through a month's snowstorms–to have shot such a creature was an era in my imagination, from which, had nature been more prodigal, I might have sprung up a poet. I trembled with a sort of fear to behold him lying indeed dead on the beach. The cold waste of water in the grey morning light, the mighty foreign bird whose plumage I had hardly ever hoped to touch but in a dream, lying like the ghost of something that ought not to have been destroyed. The scene was altogether such as made the heart quake, and almost repent of having killed a creature so surpassingly beautiful."

But that was a fleeting fancy. Sitting upon a heap of seaweed, with a swan on either side of me, I smoked and mused until the tide turned, when, sculling homeward on the flood, I reached the inn at breakfast time, with a feeling of triumph that can be better imagined than described.

> *Clanging from northern climes they cleave the sky,*
> *Intently followed by the fowler's eye;*
> *To yon lone harbour's mouth they wing their way,*
> *The five descend—and two are doomed to stay!*

CHANCE OF A LIFETIME

By "September Red"

It was in Christmas week, some long years ago, that it started to freeze and freeze, so much that the receding tide even froze on the sand and rocks. Never before, so the old folks said, had there been such a frost in those parts, certainly not for a very great number of years, then the snow started to fall.

For several days I had been away down on the marshes which covered many hundreds of acres alongside the shore line, some sand dunes intervening, for the evening flight. Although we wildfowlers waited for the frosts and hard weather to come, this intense frost did not bring the expected sport, for no doubt the birds flew far inland to where they could find some fresh water that was not frozen completely over. There were, however, no end of duck on the sea, while on the shore and mud flats there were hundreds upon hundreds of the waders, to say nothing of the geese, mostly up to then, brents.

The sport had been most disappointing until the coming of

the snow, and then for one morning's flight it was, anyway for me, unique. The snow started early on the Wednesday but no one could get out to the marshes that night as there was also a gale of wind from the east which resulted in a first class blizzard, it would not have been possible to shoot even if one had got out. I made up my mind, all being well, to turn out early next morning and somehow get to my favourite spot before daylight.

Just after four a.m. I cooked myself a good breakfast, collected my gun and cartridges, more of the latter than I could comfortably carry, in addition to my heavy clothing, and an old, small, short handled shovel which I slung over my shoulders. Opening the door I was greeted with an avalanche of snow which cascaded indoors, this was a nuisance; wasted valuable time, for I had to shovel it outside again. However, at last I got going.

It had stopped snowing but was still blowing hard. There appeared to be little frost. When I got clear of the house I found that the snow was about a foot or more deep on the flat, while the drifts were feet high in places. Obviously it was going to be a tough job to get out to the marshes, but I had luckily allowed plenty of time for that mile and a half walk. Everything appeared to be exactly right for a great morning's flight, as the tide was high just about daylight, which meant the fowl had got to fly somewhere as there would be no shore for them; further, the sea was really rough and the chances were that the duck would also come in.

Finally I reached my favourite spot by an old bit of wall which was at the tail end of a large stretch of fresh water, now, of course, frozen over and covered deep in snow, though luckily for me the wind had blown a lot of the snow over to the other side. I set to work with my little shovel and eventually had managed to clear quite a nice little patch. I would have liked to have been able to break the ice, but that was quite impossible for it was far too thick. I knew however that the fowl, if any flew in, would quickly spot the cleared space.

By the time I dug out the drift which covered my bit of wall it was beginning to get a little lighter away to the east. One could not hear anything beyond the screech of the wind as I crouched down waiting. After a while I began to get very chilly, for I had got terribly hot struggling out there through the drifts. I decided there was time to have a quick move round before anything was likely to happen, but I was wrong! There I was, right out in the open, when a large flock of wigeon came in and dived down to the cleared spot of ice and passed a few feet over my head! They were so close to me when I first realised that they were there, that I never got a shot at them.

Getting back to my hole in the snow by the wall, I had not long to wait before things began to happen. In came the ducks of all kinds, not in ones and twos, but in their hundreds, and as it got lighter great flocks of golden plover, sandpipers, curlew and some snipe came flying over, and round and round. In the white and frozen world they did not seem to know where to go to, nor did they pay any attention to me. The geese flew very high that morning and eventually went away inland, though one or two remained to be picked up later. It was the most wonderful morning's flight of wildfowl that I have ever seen, so much so that I just did not know which bird to shoot at first.

The tremendous wind kept most of them flying low and they would come in from the sea, circle round, dive down towards the clearing on the ice, rocket up and away back over the sea; and this apparently they kept on doing until the tide ebbed back and allowed them once again standing room on the shore.

To begin with I shot abominably badly, but managed to pull myself together after a bit. Although by now it was daylight, the actual light was very bad and to make matters rather worse it had started to snow a little again and the wind freshened up to nearly full gale force once more; however, I make no excuses, and I should have done better. I shot on until I had not a single cartridge left, and still the fowl continued to fly round.

The next job was to pick up my birds, which eventually I and my dog did, and I don't think that many were missed, but I remember I found the old shovel handy as some of the birds falling from a height into a snow drift were not too easy to recover. As it was, I had far more than I could carry so I took the first lot over to a solitary cottage which luckily was not too far away and came back for the others.

Wonderful though the morning flight had been, making it a red letter day always to be remembered, it was not that which I can still see so vividly in my mind's eye even today. Tramping along home very slowly indeed, for I confess that I had had nearly enough for the time being, I saw another gun plodding out towards me up the shore road. At first I could not make out who it was and then I saw that it was Fred, though why on earth he was so late coming out I just could not think, because he was one of the most experienced of all the local fowlers.

He was about a hundred and fifty yards away from me, when

I spotted what I at first thought were three swans coming up low behind him. As they got nearer, I saw that they were Canada geese! I shouted and then Fred spotted them. Up went his gun, and I waited for at least one of the great birds to come toppling down–but nothing happened! They just swerved away from him slightly and carried on. He hadn't got his gun loaded!

They flew too wide for me, and in any case I hadn't a cartridge left; but Fred had let three of them pass over him at a range of somewhere about twenty yards. The chance of a lifetime thrown away. Every now and then someone would get one of these geese which were, of course, probably strays from some park, maybe hundreds of miles away, but we always talked about them and hoped that we might be the lucky gun, the next time one happened down our way. Only once since then have I seen a Canada goose in flight and that was not within shot.

IN QUEST OF THE PINK–FOOTED GOOSE

By John Hodgson 1947

Wildfowlers in general and goose hunters in particular take a great delight in discussing their past exploits and the prospects for the future. This propensity grows stronger as the shooting season approaches and, in my case at any rate, generally leads to a visit to some favourite spot where at one time or another issue has been joined with the wily geese. Thus one warm and sunny evening during last summer I sat on the top of a five barred gate surveying a forty acre field of wheat, which shone like gold in the evening sun. Facing west I could see within half a mile the shimmering silver waters of Morecambe Bay. Behind me were the heather clad Bleasdale Fells, outriders of the more distant Pennines. It was a scene to delight the eye of the country lover. I wished that it could be seen by some of the thousands of folk who think that Lancashire is a land of factory chimneys and clogs and shawls.

As I gazed over the sea of waving wheat my mind slipped back to a morning in December last when the outlook was very different. On that occasion, before daylight, my wildfowling friend, Dickie, and I crept silently down the old lane, the only sound being the dull thud of our rubber boots on the frozen surface. We were making for the big field on which, according to information received from the kindly farmer, a large flock of pink-footed geese had fed daily for the past week. We reached the field, which is roughly rectangular in shape, in time to smoke a cigarette before dawn. As the sky paled in the east we looked over the ground, which was half barley stubble and the remainder clover, the dividing line being a shallow trough or dyke, left, no doubt, by some draining operation. The middle portion of the field was covered with goose droppings, some of which were so fresh that we felt certain the geese would come. We then dispersed to our positions, Dickie selecting a point at the dyke end, half way along the easterly boundary, whilst I got down in the cover of the hedge in the corner nearest to the sea, from which direction I knew the geese would come, if they came at all.

It was bitterly cold. We had been in our positions perhaps half an hour when I heard the distant calling of the geese. I sank down into the hedge bottom to watch a skein of about thirty geese come nearer and nearer. On they came, their clamorous music ever louder. My heart thumped with excitement as I watched them draw closer but, alas! They came in wide and well out of shot. They circled the middle of the field several times and, as they did so, the calling ceased. I knew that two gimlet eyes in each head were straining to detect any danger below. Evidently satisfied they planed in to land, when a babble of noise started again, only to subside when they began to feed.

Within a few minutes more geese were heard and a smaller flock, being decoyed by those already down, pitched straight into the middle of the field without any preliminaries, but again out of shot. Two further lots came. We were then in the position of being within sight of perhaps a hundred feeding geese but, as I thought, powerless to do anything about it. I took out my binoculars for a close-up view of the birds. From my slightly higher position I observed Dickie 'belly crawling' up the shallow dyke, which I had thought was not deep enough to hide a cat. He was perfectly flat. I knew that if any man could get at the birds it was my companion, who can make himself nearly invisible when it comes to stalking geese.

Slowly he drew nearer. When he was within perhaps fifty yards of the nearest birds I saw first one and then another head raised, and then, with a mighty clamour they were up. There came two reports as the 8 bore belched four and a half ounces of BB shot. One goose dropped, another left the main flock, a sure sign that it was hit. I lost interest in Dickie, for a party of about eight geese were coming straight for me. They veered away at about forty yards, but one, slightly nearer than the rest, fell stone dead to the choke barrel of my magnum twelve. I gathered my goose and chased across to Dickie, to find him wet through to the skin and his clothes already freezing upon him. He announced that he had seen his second goose come down a couple of fields away. In due course we recovered this also. These were not the first geese, by a long way, that we had brought to the bag during a long companionship, but the thrill of success in this wildest and grandest sport with the gun, carried on within sound of the sea, is always new. We were two very satisfied mortals as we carried our bag back up the old lane, where frost covered hedgerows were now glistening in the morning sun.

AN OLD WILDFOWLER.

A Wildfowlers Symphony.

There is a time when to the lonely man
All movement seems suspended for a while
And in the marshlands silence reigns supreme
While light remains, although the sun has set.
He may be tired, cold and weary, wet
But still he'll find a solace in the quiet
Until the silence breaks . . . .

A drumming snipe
Shatters the mirror surface of the calm,
Ghostly, invisible, near enough to touch.
This is the prelude . . . .

Light has nearly gone
And peeweets' pleading notes sound all around:
They flutter by on wings that seem to creak
Too low to see except for fleeting glance.
A great white owl drifts across the moor.
They should be coming soon. . . .
Wheeoo, Wheeoo.
The cold hands tighten and the gun comes up.
Chirping and chattering with fast whistling wings,
Shadows of shadows in the now dark sky,

The flighting widgeon seek the flooded moors.
One shot, a boom, an eight-bore probably;
A single, heavy, leaden lifeless splash
And then the frenzied splashings of a dog:
Some fowler has a dinner to take home.
Pochard and pintail, mallard, shoveller, teal
Are mingling with the widgeon as they fly:
The sky is filled with noises and with wings.
The birds are settling in and quiet now,
Save for the quacking of some distant mallard,

They seek their feed. . . .

The moon is rising,
Long golden rays reach out across the moor
And trees show stark against the eastern sky.
Now is the grand finale. . . .
A clarion in the sky,
Tensing, arresting, thrilling to the core,
The baying of some supernatural hounds,
Or wild celestial laughter of the gods;
So do the pinkfeet herald their approach.
Now great dark shadows sweep across the moon
And gunners strain their eyes into the night,
Seeking the prize most coveted of all.

FOURTEEN RULES FOR PUNT-GUNNERS.

By. Sir Ralph Payne-Gallwey. (1887)

Let the fowler when seeking sport:

Avoid following, or firing at, birds during high water, or even when the ooze beds are covered by the tide. There is great risk of driving the birds from their feeding grounds and making them wild and restless. If fowl are left in peace at high water, they will merely float about near or over the beds of ooze they feed on when the tide is out. They then get a haunt, and a good shot at them will sooner or later be obtainable.

Do not endeavour to set up to wildfowl in a punt unless pretty sure you can float up in range, as the action consequent on struggling and pushing over a shallow will usually alarm the birds, when by waiting a short time the flowing tide might easily have permitted a near approach and a certain shot.

Shooting on the ebb tide is on nineteen out of twenty occasions a waste of time, and a loss of birds; for the same birds might have been obtained on the flood, when there would probably be water to float nearly up to them. If fowl are left in peace on the ooze when it is uncovered by the ebb, they will often sleep and feed, and becoming quiet and confident in consequence, allow the punter to get in shot of them as he floats quickly up with the flood tide.

If the fowl rise time after time just out of range, settle, and rise again every time they are set to, they are well on the alert. Do not fancy for a moment that because they pitch again not far distant they ignore your presence, or that they are but naturally restless and will in time settle down and afford a shot. Nothing of the kind. You might follow them all day till your arms ached, and yet obtain not even the remotest chance. It rather shows that if they were left alone for several hours they might quiet down, though this they would never do so long as your punt was within a couple of miles, or at all events in sight of them.

The harder it blows the better for punting, always provided your punt can live in the sea knocked up by the wind, and also that you can steer and shoot in it. If you can get near them, you will find all wildfowl unusually tame in a gale of wind, as they dislike riding it out in the tossing waves, and when on the ooze sit huddled together for mutual shelter from the blast that would otherwise ruffle their feathers.

The best hour to look for a shot is at dawn, that is, if the feeding grounds which the fowl frequent are just being covered by the tide at that time. The birds, having been on the feed all night, are heavy and loath to take wing, especially so if, feeding over the last bit of ooze, they have no chance of finding more food till the next ebb again uncovers it.

The most favourable time to seek a shot by day is about an hour before low water. You will then most probably be at your shooting grounds at low water, and therefore ready to take a chance at fowl with the first of the flood, or at once to set at birds that may happen to be resting on the outermost edge of the ooze banks, before the tide, one way or the other, affects your approach.

It is the rule in most places that spring tides are the best for punting, and especially so when high water is at eleven o'clock in the day, as then there is a good chance of a shot both morning and evening. Low water at three o'clock is very suitable for afternoon shooting, high water at ten o'clock for early morning sport, or under a late moon.

Shooting by night is a hopeless undertaking, unless the moon be bright, the sky clear, and the weather still. It is also generally useless to try and shoot birds swimming by night. They should be found and fired at on the ooze. The young fowler must give up all idea of seeing or approaching birds by night, except by going directly towards the light of the moon; in fact, he should get between himself and the moon, and so in the rays of the latter; any other way of setting to fowl by night is a waste of time. If he come on the birds with the moon behind him, they will see his punt a couple of hundred yards distant and fly away, whilst he would not see them thirty yards off, even were they not to leave. He may hear birds calling all round him, some apparently within a few yards, but never a shot will he get, except at those in the bright reflection of the moon as he paddles towards that luminary. It is not much use trying for fowl early in the night, as at that time they are spread all over their feeding grounds in open order, like crows in a field, scarcely two being together, however numerous they may be collectively. About an hour before dawn, if the tide be a little over half flood, and the moon fairly bright, is the best hour for a night shot. The birds will by that time have gradually fed together and become packed as the tide surrounds both them and their food; they are then favourably placed for a shot if they can be properly set to against the light of the moon, or towards the first glint of daylight in the sky. The most suitable shot to use at night is No. 2, as if a shot can then be got at all it is usually a pretty close one.

Distance is a great source of trouble to a young fowler. Seventy yards is a fair range for a punt gun, though sixty is a better and gives less cripples, but without considerable practice it is hard to judge accurately a distance of seventy yards across water, as to a novice a hundred yards appear no more than fifty or sixty. Practice alone makes perfect in this respect.

Above all things check any excitement, or undue anxiety when drawing in shot of fowl. If the shot is to be had, well and good; if not, all the anxiety in your nature will not give it to you. Excitement or anxiety usually means restless movements, such as peeping over the gunwale of the punt every few moments to see what the birds are doing. The slightest suspicious motion is instantly observed by wildfowl, and it is the fact that their suspicion is aroused that causes them to be instantly, and afterwards continually, watchful against approach, whereas if you had remained motionless as to your head and eyes, steadily paddling on meanwhile, the birds might not have taken alarm till too late for their safety.

If in shot, fire the instant the fowl raise their heads, and they will spring at the flash and meet the shot with their wings spread; you can always paddle on so long as the birds have not stretched their necks.

You will have to act as quick as thought when you do fire: One second too late and instead of a score of birds you may have none. It may appear easy to send a charge fairly into a hundred birds at sixty yards, but it is not, and the most experienced fowlers often miss, especially if the punt (as is often the case) is dancing about on rippling water, tiny waves, maybe, but still quite large and lively enough to make aiming a gun eight feet long, as the gunner lies close in his punt, an uncertain business.

If you are fortunate enough to knock over some birds, row up to them as quickly as possible and keep your eyes on those that fly away for "droppers" out of the pack, for there are sure to be some that fall at a distance if you made anything of a successful shot. Shoot the furthermost cripples first and those near or on the shore next, using the shoulder gun for this purpose; the dead birds are comparatively safe, and can be picked up last of all.

Finally, let me repeat that wildfowl shooting with punt and gun is of all sports the most uncertain. The fowl may be visible in thousands, but that is no proof they are to be obtained, and we have usually done more execution on small numbers of birds than on large, for in large packs there are so many more bright peering eyes to see danger than where the fowl are less numerous. Do not therefore be disappointed at your ill luck at first. No amount of hard work or skill will command success in punting if the fates be against you, though there may be always the promise of good sport. In the vista of years we remember our good fortune and are apt to forget the many, many, blank days we have had after wildfowl, for there are miserable failures as well as glorious successes in this kind of sport.

AN EARLY WIGEON FLIGHT

By "Sinbad"

The rough low lying meadows, not far inland from the coast and a broad, sheltered estuary, had lain under snow and then been flooded; then they had frozen over but were now thawed once more, leaving only the shallow flashes so beloved of wigeon, through which the tops of the grasses protruded. One field, somewhat higher than its neighbours, had yielded a good crop of potatoes and now, soggy and wet, was rich with gleanings. Between this and the best of the lower flooded land ran a brimful and rush girt ditch about six feet wide, with at one end a tumbledown but nevertheless convenient plank bridge spanning it.

The wind was from out of the north-east, ideal for this particular place, and we, the two gunners, after surveying the scene and sniffing the breeze decided to station ourselves on the edge of the ditch about two hundred yards apart. As we seperated the last of the gulls winged their way lazily westwards; their garrulous company were dispersing for the night. The

116

time was about four o'clock of a late December afternoon; a moon in its second quarter rode the sky. The wind was quite fresh, although not so strong as we could have wished it, but it carried with it an abundance of low fleecy clouds; conditions we had prayed for. From time immemorial these meadows have been a favourite resort of wildfowl; the surface feeders, teal, mallard and wigeon could always be expected and even– upon rare occasions–a few geese attracted by the potatoes. But now it was wigeon we were most interested in.

By four-twenty the light had almost gone, the willows at the far end of the ditch had assumed witch-like proportions, and one could have sworn that they moved hither and thither, waving their skinny arms. A grey mistiness enshrouded the inland scene whilst the long flood wall in front loomed dark and bastion like against the fading grandeur of the western sky. The sun had sunk suddenly from sight, vast and dull red as it disappeared behind a cloud mass; its after glow washed pale cold green; flecked with pink and orange tinted cloudlets, into deep brown and sombre purple haze. Darkness enfolded us, the land was hushed yet expectant.

A peewit called, and several came twisting and tumbling, borne on the path of the wind; so often the first-comers at flight time. Curlew were about, their plaintive notes enhancing;

from out of the distance, the solitude; from close at hand sounded the harsh *scaape-scaape*! of the first snipe to flit by unseen. A faint whirr of wings, a tiny splash, and one of them lets within five yards of me, as I sit, a muffled, quiet figure on an upturned bucket in the reeds by the ditch: it is oblivious of, or unconcerned by my presence. From the farmland behind, partridges *chuk-chuk* as they settle down for the night.

The stage is set. A tinkling thrumming of fast beating wings announces all of a sudden the arrival of the first of the teal as a bunch of five streak by overhead: two thunderous reports shatter the silence. My companion down by the bridge has gone into action; to be answered by the cries and calls of alarm as a host of unsuspected birds take wing all around us. A moorhen croaks derisively from the safety of the reeds, for those teal have passed on unharmed. Someone upwind and out of sight by the flood wall, whistles a tune as he makes his way homewards, the notes of a popular song sound thin and incongruous over the keen air. A distant train puffs importantly from the little Halt two miles away.

Whicker and whisper of wings, teal again tinkle by. Then comes a more sibilant note and the voices of mallard, the heavy duck are now on the move. Several drop down on to the potato field where, although invisible to us, they can be heard guzzling and talking. *Swi-swi-swi-swi-swi-swi*! More pinions rustle on high, and I peer around straining my eyes for a sight of the birds. *Bang-bang!* . . . . *Bang*! My friend spots them first and I get in a single shot as they go rocketing past; a splashing thud behind me providing a pleasing assurance of at least one down.

W'whee-ou! Wheeou! From somewhere out of the sky comes the un-duck-like but heart gripping whistle of wigeon, then again. Now seven graceful shapes are silhouetted momentarily clear against the moonlit cloud; they turn and come in as we both wait breathlessly for them to come lower. They are too far for me but my companion fires twice. And as the crash of the explosions fades I hear two thuds; has he pulled off a right and left or two birds to one shot? The remaining five vanish, hurtling upwards and out of sight.

Again and again those lovely whistles float earthwards as the cocks streak in, whilst behind them and much more subdued, sounds the purring growl of the females. The sky is full of their voices; this is a night of nights. Shot after shot reverberates over the meadows until, as though at a signal, the flight ends and silence clamps down. It has been a full hour and a quarter of thrilling excitement, an occasion to store in the memory. The fallen are gathered—as many as possible having been picked as they were shot—and the tramp back across the water logged fields begins. Jet, the old labrador bitch, runs in to shot, but that can be an advantage at this sort of game when the pick-up is often so chancy an affair. She has proved her worth on many a night and must be cared for as soon as the car is reached and she can be rubbed down.

The moon now hangs unobscured in the cloudless steel-blue night, the stars wink and flash as the newly formed ice crackles underfoot; frost grips hedgerow, thicket and ditch. The barn, sheltering the car, glimmers strange and unreal, criss-crossed by grotesque shadows thrown by an oak. The wind has veered, bringing back intense cold which will seal in ice those wigeon flashes back on the meadows. We have been lucky, for there will be no more inland flight there until the next thaw.

Thus the impressions of a foray after wigeon; and what of one's thoughts as one waits, cold and expectant, for the first sound of their magical voices? That night I pondered of duck flighting in general and a fault my companion was over prone to. It has so often surprised me how some men, who should know a great deal better, will persist in over shooting some favourite flight haunt. Wild duck are indeed wild birds; it is quite unreasonable to expect them to stand up to incessant attack. One realises full well the temptation; it is nice if a successful outing can be repeated; one is anxious to go out again the next night, but it is unwise in the end. The "lead in" will be broken sooner or later and birds, at all events in any numbers, will be unlikely to frequent the same place as before.

When a good flight pond or permanent flash has been found–and maybe enhanced by a little judicial feeding–duck should be first left in peace to establish their lead in. The place may then be shot, but thereafter should be left for a fortnight, or certainly a week. That this calls for self control and patience is undoubted (should not that be part of the 'fowler's make-up?), but it will give better results in the long run. It is foolish and short sighted to go out night after night, bang away, and expect to continue success. The man who does so misjudges his quarry and defeats his own ends; but it is astonishing how some will persist in this folly.

STANCHION
GUN BARRELS AND THEIR MAKERS

By Captain Lacy (1842)

My largest stanchion-gun barrel was forged under my own
eye, entirely of dray stubs, by the late renowned Tom Fullerd,
of London. But poor Tom, like Tom Bowling, Tom Moody,
and other matchless Toms, hath now, alas! gone the way of
all flesh; and with him hath fallen the once so flourishing
establishment in Compton Street.

Mr. Daniel and Colonel Hawker have deservedly eulogized
the Fullerds. And Tom in particular, as "London barrel maker
in chief;" and as the Colonel has also composed the epitaph
of the late Joe Manton, I would humbly hope that the ashes
of poor Tom, who made so many in his time, will not be
permitted to sleep unmemorialized. "Here lies Fuller(d)'s
earth," is surely not enough. And, by way of endeavouring to
induce the Colonel, or some other competent person, to take
up his pen in last eulogy of this prince of barrel forgers, my
willing muse, shall essay a brief epitaph on another celebrated

man:-

> *"No longer seek his merits to descant on,*
> *A noble man lies here—honest Joe Manton."*

The best advice I have to offer to any modern shooter, desirous of obtaining a first rate large gun barrel, is, to get it either direct, or through his gunmaker, from Birmingham, where a good many artists are to be found competent to the undertaking, and, among them, none, perhaps, more so than Mr. John Clive, Mr. Joseph Turner, or Mr. March. Perhaps the best plan is to send a model of the barrel, turned in wood, showing the exact proportions you have decided upon, with exact size of bore, &c.; and it is best to have the barrel fine bored before it is proved, or leaves Birmingham, as no gunmaker out of that town, at least that I know (except Purdey) has convenience or implements for boring large guns.

The reducing, cupping, and touching the plug, are always left for the gunmaker to execute; the barrel forger never does these things, except at an extra charge; and it is far better to employ your own gunmaker. These may be, and I doubt not there are, many other gunmakers competent to get up a large gun, with Colonel Hawker's apparatus attached to it; but Mr. Purdey of London, and Mr. Edge of Manchester, are the best I know of at present; and it may be observed that these guns cannot be well got up at a small expense.

My large barrel is, I believe, as good a piece of workmanship as ever emanated from the forge of a Fullerd; yet I have reason to imagine that it was about the last of that stamp turned out from the old establishment, which, latterly, was not what it once was; nor would mine have been the gun it is, but for extra surveillance and extra cost. Whilst, therefore, in justice to the living and the dead, I should recommend that the latest works of Tom be disregarded by the young gunner, who may have a chance of purchase, yet those which bear the initials of William Fullerd, and which can be ascertained to be "undoubted originals," if not internally injured—and the breech should be taken off to examine them—are highly to be prized. They are all forged exclusively of English or foreign stubs, and will stand a proof far beyond that which the proof house requires. No man ever had a more efficient set of workmen, or was better furnished with the means and appliances for conducting his business, or had greater pride in turning out first rate workmanship, than the late William Fullerd, who, unfortunately for his brother Tom, died before him, and much too early.

Before I dismiss the present subject, there is one point upon which I deem it necessary to dwell–I allude to what are called the single and double fortified plans of forging large barrels. The single fortification is where a barrel is forged of common iron throughout, except about two feet from the breech end, which is formed of stub iron, twisted. The advantage of this is obvious, inasmuch as the greatest strain, or pressure upon the barrel, is here from the sudden, and, as it were, local expansion of the powder, and where, also, the shot first lifts. The double fortification is where the barrel is, as usual, single twist throughout, but double twisted for a foot or two only, at the breech end. Thus, instead of forging these last two feet in one piece, or spiral, the full thickness required, two lengths of spirals, reversely twisted (those of the intended inside case, to the left; and of the outside case, to the right), are separately forged, and then the joints of each, being separately closed in a welding heat, the two cases being placed on the mandrel, one above the other, are closely welded together.

But in the forging of my large gun, I went beyond this; for I had it doubly fortified throughout, i.e. from breech to muzzle. In other words, this is encasing and welding together two single-stub reversely-twisted barrels in one. What can burst this? At the same time, in having recourse to this plan, I had another object in view, besides the security of the barrel; I thereby hoped, also, to obtain an inside cleaner from "blacks" and "grays" than is usual in large guns; and in this I certainly succeeded; for no small gun has a more polished inside throughout, or one more entirely free from specks, than my large one.

The nearer the hammer the better the iron; because, as the blow is the more forcible there, so are the pores of the iron the most closely condensed; and hence it follows that a barrel forged according to the process just named, must receive the condensing power of the hammer in, at the least, a two-fold degree; and hence, too, when the boring-bit has removed all the "blacks" and begins to taste the best of the iron, just when we have got the bore to the desired size, and the smoothing and finishing process is about to be given to the interior, we have also just reached the very best of the iron, where it is the most desirable that such should be; namely on the inner side of the barrel. We have nearly reached the exterior—or what, before the welding, was the exterior—of the innermost case; have cut within a few shavings of the outer rind of the orange, without having damaged its golden covering; and thus the inside of the barrel will wear like a piece of steel!

But whilst I recommend the double fortification for two feet at the breech-end, for every large stanchion-gun barrel, I do not consider the double fortification throughout of moment to any but the very largest; and then, only, when you are desirous of having a something highly finished in the large way.

As regards "the loop" belonging to Colonel Hawker's apparatus, this must either be forged on to the barrel, as he himself recommends, or must be fixed on it afterwards; and, for my own part, I prefer the latter. But, whichever plan be adopted, the grand point is, to fix the loop on the proper part of the barrel, so that when the swivel is home in the stanchion, the muzzle-end of the gun shall have a preponderance of, say twenty pounds. Recollect, if the loop be placed too far back, you will need a cannon-metal stock, or loaded butt, to counterbalance the extra weight forwards, so as to enable you to elevate the gun with proper ease; and if the same be placed too far forwards, there will be an injurious preponderance in the opposite extreme, so that the muzzle, instead of resting on the deck, as it ought to do, will always be elevated far above it.

The largest gun barrel I ever heard of, was manufactured by Mr. March, in Birmingham. It was some nine feet six inches long, some two inches and a half in bore, and weighed three hundred weight; and so *grilling* a job did it prove, that the foreman of the fire assured me he "would not undertake the making another such–not if any one would keep him for nothing for the remainder of his life!" This barrel (intended, I understood, for a very distinguished gunner in the south) was single twist, which as far as I could learn, the Birmingham forgers (contrary to the Fullerd's and the late Joe Manton's notions) consider preferable to double. All large barrels, when nearly finished as to boring and grinding, should be hammer hardened for a great length of time; and may afterwards be turned in a sliding lathe.

In forging these ponderous barrels, nothing adds momentum to the fall of the hammer so certainly as double stout, applied internally at judicious intervals: for, in all good truth, the employment is nothing else, from first to last, but a combination of the most grilling heat with the hardest labour; it is even worse than anchor-forging, because, in the latter, more time is allowed the hammer men between "the heats."

A stanchion-gun should always have a back actioned lock. As the springs of the lock are liable to fly in frosty weather, they should be long and not too high tempered. To prevent losing sport, it is advisable to have a duplicate by you, especially as, in case of accident, you may have to send a long distance to get the other lock repaired. The lock plate should be well chamfered to keep the wet out, though a waterproof lock cover should at all times be used. Springs of any kind, on the outside of a lock to be used on salt water are objectionable and particularly so when they cannot be easily got at to be properly cleaned. The lock plate should be thick, and about half as large again as that for a large shoulder duck gun, for nothing is more absurd than the common idea that a large stanchion-gun must have a lock in proportion to its size: hence some of these locks are perfect monsters.

SOME FORGOTTEN EDIBLE BIRDS

By H.A. Bryden (1904)

The list of British birds which were formerly esteemed as delicacies by our forefathers is, when one begins to look into the matter, by no means an inconsiderable one. Some of these birds, such as ruffs and reeves, have fallen out of fashion owing to the melancholy fact that they are nowadays no longer attainable. The drainage of the fens and the advances of cultivation have practically banished them from these islands. In other cases the disappearance of certain birds from modern cookery books and the tables of gourmets and the well to do is not so easily explainable.

Wheatears, for example, had somehow lost their high place in the estimation of *bons vivants* for some time before the introduction of the Wild Birds Protection Acts of the last twenty three years. Yet wheatears were, and still are, undoubtedly, a great delicacy, well comparable, as they used to be, with the ortolan of the Continent. Under their present blessed state of immunity from capture, very few, indeed, of these birds are tasted in this country, and they are now never seen in poulterers shops, as they used to be until a few years back in certain Sussex coast towns.

The South Down shepherds have perforce, given up snaring them, and although here and there some epicure may procure on the quiet a dozen or two of these dainties for his own private consumption, they are now practically unknown on English tables. These birds are in their prime in September, just as they leave our shores, when, fattened and recruited by their summer sojourn in mellow England, they are–I suppose one must say "were"–undoubtedly, delicious eating. Still, tempting as they are, I prefer the sight of these cheerful migrants, with their handsome plumage, and quick, restless, flirting ways, their tolerance of mankind, and their pleasant little song, to the same creatures baked, like so many blackbirds, in a capacious pie.

Ruffs and reeves have, like the wheatear vanished from the kitchens of British cooks and the tables of the rich. Unlike those birds, however, they are at the present day very seldom found in these islands except occasionally as mere passing visitants on their spring and summer migrations. In the days when they were plentiful they were netted by the aid of decoys, and thereafter fattened for about a fortnight, being fed on boiled wheat, and bread and milk, mixed with hemp seed and occasionally sugar. Thus prepared, they were considered by our ancestors among the greatest delicasies that could be offered to a distinguished guest.

The bar tailed godwit, known locally as the yarwhelp, sea woodcock, and half-curlew, is another of the great family of wading birds which was formerly in much estimation as a table luxury. It was taken in nets by means of stuffed decoys, much as were ruffs and reeves, and commanded a high price. *The Field Book*, published in the early thirties of the last century, describes it as "a bird of peculiar delicacy." Although fairly common during the spring and autumn migrations, this godwit is now but little known except to marsh and shore gunners, and its undoubted merits as a table bird seem to have passed into oblivion.

Yet another wader, the dainty knot, a much smaller bird than the godwit, which weighs as much as twelve ounces, has become a table bird almost completely forgotten. Yet the knot, was until a century or so ago, captured in much the same manner in the fen country, fattened in the same way for sale, and as much esteemed by many as its bigger cousin, the ruff. Knots are still frequently seen round our coasts, in some seasons in large numbers. Sir Ralph Payne-Gallwey, one of the greatest and keenest of modern wildfowlers, bagged, not many years since, as many as a hundred and sixty of these birds at a single discharge of his punt gun.

Among other waders which apparently were looked upon by our ancestors as good table birds, were the redshank, curlew, dunlin and bittern. In the time of Henry VIII. the redshank was priced at the value of a penny, at which rate teal and widgeon were then sold. In 1833 the market value was from a shilling to fifteen pence, which seems to indicate that the redshank is a bird of considerably higher table value than many people suppose. The greenshank, a much rarer bird in England than its cousin the redshank, is also well flavoured as to its flesh, and used to be esteemed very good eating.

Dunlin, or ox-birds, known to our predecessors of Henry VIII. 's time, and even now by the country folk of various districts as "sturts," or "struts," and "purres," were in 1512 rated at the value of 6d a dozen. In 1833 poulterers priced them at the rate of 3d apiece. Dunlin, however, besides being excessively tiny morsels when stripped of their plumage, are not particularly good eating, and at the present time are seldom tasted except by the poorer class of shore shooters and fisher folk. Curlew, valued at 12d. in 1512, and at 2s. in 1833, are but poor things as table birds; and at their best, however, during summer time, when living inland and feeding on the moors, they are just passable. When their diet is a seashore one their flesh is rank and unpleasant. Stints were certainly eaten by our forefathers, and in a Yorkshire estate book of 1760 are priced at only half a penny less than snipe, which are set down in the same book as 2d. apiece.

The stone curlew, or Norfolk plover–otherwise known as the thick knee plover–is a bird of remarkable excellence from the culinary point of view. It is, however, a scarce bird in this country and is sheltered very properly by the Wild Birds Protection Acts during a great part of its sojurn with us. I have tasted many a time in South Africa the "dikkop" (literally thick-head, a Boer name), which is a very near relative of our British stone curlew. In appearance there is very little difference between these two large plovers. Both have the curiously rounded heads, large, protruding eyes–in the one case yellow, in the other (the South African) yellowish green–pale tawny brown mottled plumage, light underneath, long legs, and curiously swollen knee joints. Both have the same squatting, crouching habits, the bird preferring rather to lie flattened completely on the soil, with the object–which by the way, it often achieves–of escaping the gunner's eye, rather than mount the air and make use of its wings. So good was the flesh of the South African thick-knee that we preferred this bird to all the bustards, save only the great *paauw* and Stanley bustard, and to most of the francolins or African partridges. Seventy years ago the market price of the Norfolk plover was no more than three shillings, so that it must have been then fairly plentiful.

Green plover or lapwing, of course, we still eat, as also the delicious golden plover. I am afraid those uninitiated in the characteristics of these birds have, pretty frequently in London restaurants, the peewit palmed off upon them instead of that much rarer delicacy, the golden plover. There is one infallible test by which the diner out may settle the question of species. The right golden plover (*pluvier dore*) of the bills of fare has no hind toe, while the common green plover possesses that appendage. A glance at the feet of the bird placed before the diner will at once inform him whether he is putting his fork into a choice tit-bit or a very ordinary table bird. The grey plover, a very beautiful British bird, is also extremely good eating; but is now so scarce as to be seldom secured even by discriminating shore shooters.

The dotterel, a now rare species of the plover kind, is yet another bird to be classed among our lost luxuries of the table. Formerly netted by our ancestors in large numbers, it is now one of our scarcest spring and summer migrants, and is seldom set eyes upon, except by those who are close observers and watch very carefully in May or early June for its rare appearances.

In 1512 cranes were valued at sixteen pence apiece, a considerable sum in those days. It is difficult to understand how our forefathers could have extracted any kind of pleasure from the flesh of this bird, or from that of the heron, which was at that same period priced at twelve pence. The bittern, valued also at twelve pence and in 1833 at from five shillings to seven shillings would scarcely be regarded at the present time, even if it were common, as a bird likely to lend itself to good eating.

The great bustard, that prince of edible sporting birds was always in much demand. Once a much and deservedly esteemed dainty on English tables, it is now, perforce, from the very rarity of its occurrence, a quite forgotten bird. Of old the pride of the banquet of many a high, noble, and well acred squire, its fame is now no other than a mere tradition among us. Yet, until the beginning of the last century, these birds were familiar to British sportsmen. So lately as the year 1808, near the estate of Mr. W.T. St. Quintin, on the Yorkshire wolds, by aid of a stalking horse and a big fowling piece, a gamekeeper to that gentleman secured no less than eleven of these magnificent birds as the result of a single discharge. Seven fell dead at once, while four others were gathered afterwards. In those days the equipment of a keeper on the wild Yorkshire wolds consisted of a trained stalking horse, a coat made from the skin of a dead horse, with the hair outside, and a mighty gun—no doubt a 4-bore. Number 3 shot were used, and the stalker often got within thirty yards of his game. With this outfit the bustards, which in those days bred in this locality, were successfully circumvented.

The water rail is by no means bad eating, and the moorhen, properly cooked, is well worth sending to table. The moorhen, in fact, is by no means a despisable quantity from the culinary point of view. I have heard of a certain yeoman, who understood good living as well as most people, who declared that he preferred one of these birds to a partridge any day.

The coot, so common a wildfowl in many inland waters, is not, nowadays, a bird often utilised for the food of English folk, except among poorer country people who have not the opportunity of attaining better fare. Yet at one time it was beyond doubt largely eaten even among the middle classes. Colonel Montagu, the ornithologist, who wrote at the beginning of the last century, says of this bird "Vast flocks are seen in Southampton river, and other salt water inlets, in winter. At this season of the year it is commonly sold in our markets, frequently ready picked. They look exceedingly white, but the flavour is rather fishy." I have tasted coot, and can endorse this statement. Some of the fishy savour can be mitigated by skinning the bird and by long immersion in cold water, which should be repeatedly changed. It is also stated that to get the best results in the way of cooking the bird should be shot early in the day. Sir Ralph PayneGallwey, a great authority on wildfowl, says that when coots first appear on the coast in winter from their inland haunts they are excellent eating. That seems to me somewhat high praise for this bird. To prepare coots for the table they should be plucked, then well rubbed with rosin, after dipping in boiling water. By this means the troublesome black down is got rid of. Then comes the immersion in cold water, which should, according to Colonel Hawker, last for twenty four hours, with frequent changes. Skinning is a troublesome process, and by some authorities is said to destroy the better flavour of the bird. "Moorhens," says Hawker, "may be cleaned in like manner (with rosin and steeping in cold water), and if in good condition. They will then be equal to any waterfowl."

GREY GOOSE SHOOTING AFLOAT

By Stanley Duncan

While the shooting of brent geese in suitable localities can be so successful afloat, the shooting of grey geese with a stanchion gun is not only disappointing, difficult and often dangerous at most of the tidal goose haunts in the British Isles, but a phase of sport both fascinating and exciting. To begin with, these wily fowl spend the night on tidal reaches where the currents run swift and strong, and where a thousand eyes constantly peer through the darkness and detect the approach of the smallest craft. By day when these birds, for various reasons, are afloat they are the most vigilant and unapproachable of all wildfowl. After many years experience I can only recollect about two, or at most three, occasions when a shot at even a small flock of grey geese on the water has been achieved; this possibly is better described as being in the half light rather than in the daylight.

Out on the open sands and wide expanses of water, a large flock of geese is ordinarily unapproachable, and sometimes, as I have seen, there can be ten thousand. To set out in a duck punt in pursuit of such quarry while the sun is up is about as hopeless as expecting to reach the moon. To succeed, close study of the habits of geese, both by day and by night, is essential, coupled with no small measure of risk and daring, for persecuted as these fowl are in most places, they display an uncanny sense of self preservation and rise at times when the punt is drawing near for no apparent reason, but they have sensed danger. Consequently, only under cover of darkness and when the weather, tide, wind and every conceivable advantage is favourable, will success attend. Even so I could recall many gooseless nights.

Wildfowlers refer to species of grey geese in relation to their wariness, declaring this is more so than that. Generally the greylag is looked upon as less wary then the pink-footed. Certainly there is no more cautious species than the latter, because everywhere in his wandering he is the object of pursuit. He is more nomadic than the greylag or the white front, or possibly all our geese, though he rarely goes to Ireland. The greylag, if chased afloat, becomes equally difficult to come to terms with, but as a species the pink footed goose, which is the commonest of all, can be a problem indeed. You could pursue them for weeks, especially on the water, and never shoot a bird, unless the fates that be cast favour in the right direction.

Eager eyes have gazed out over the leaden waters of the estuary at sundown; will the night be suitable to go after the geese? Darkness has set in, but the wind has not dropped; the tortuous boil of the swishing current gurgles along the channel as the tide flows and we feel that to go out there where the geese, drifting with the stream, are all alert and calling, would be so much waste of time. On such a night, while you might see birds, they would see you first and swim away and past, leaving you guessing where they were, and to find them rising where you least expected, far out of shot and in the wrong direction.

Hushed as by a magic hand, the still air of an October night softly wafts in gentle mist aglow from the lights across the water. Banks of fog pack on the river's shore; patches brighten in the starlit sky. It is a night of nights; the fowler knows that well. At midnight, the neap tide slowly and with sluggish impulses will fill the river's basin; the geese awakened from their watchful slumber on the sands will start calling as the water creeps around, glistening beneath the beams of light ships and beacons, rippled and turmoiled by the wake of thundering steamers, casting a glare over the water from portholes and mast lights as they proceed. Almost to our feet stretch the lights' reflections, a sure indication that a suitable night for great things is at hand. Then as the tide rises, the geese are calling out on the water, knowing also that the arch enemy,

141

man, may have advantage, for out of that bank of fog outlined with reedy fringes of the shore, may steal a foe tremendous and death dealing–the duck punt and its deadly gun.

With quickened ears we listen intently on the shore, ready to put off at a moments notice. Sounds of geese on the water ring out clearly on the night; those sounds so assuring to the practised ear that danger to their kind lurks near by; for once in a while conditions favour the men and boat. Gradually the sounds, plaintively piercing and convincing of dread, soften with distance as the fowl drift slowly towards where for centuries probably has been their stronghold of retreat–the slack water of full sea off the Bowser Light. It is time to be off.

With muffled strokes the oars pull hard across the running channel and soon midstream is reached and the shore, save for the light in our cottage window that is a guide if the mist clears, is lost to view. Soon we make upstream, for it is yet half an hour to high water. Goose calls, uneasy and restless, fearsome of danger, come from ahead. We are on the right direction. Then the curse of the situation is sighted–steamers, steamers, steamers! Dare we risk the wake and swamp? No, we must dress back. Hard pulling puts us half a mile from our course before the steamers pass, three close following, setting down to the sea still against the rising tide, putting a wake awash that would sink a lifeboat. Keeping off shore, we toss and roll, the punt stem slapping on the water with quivering thumps, keeping time to the throbbing engines of the passing steamers and the breaking wake wash on the river bank.

Tossed are the geese on the rolling surf, calling repeatedly, signalling to sit tight, steamers are no enemy! Then as calm settles, slowly the punt is moved forward, its occupants prone and motionless, tense with fear and excitement. At length the geese are sighted, a long thin line on the water; geese only as the punter sees and knows them. So placed with a background of haze and darkness, the birds seemingly cannot see the punt. Stealthily, without the slightest sound, or results might be fatal, the floating gunners move nearer and nearer, till the notes of calling geese sound close and loud.

It's time to shoot! But no! They must be up! Readjusted aim and the gun bears high. The geese at last are at the gunner's mercy. Just as a shooting star streaks across the sky, the geese have seen the enemy. For an instant not a sound is heard; a dead silence precedes a roar, and with a thousand voices that unite in an ear splitting chorus, the birds are up. It is but an act of less than a second and a boom responds to a sharp tug of the lanyard. A bright flash in the dark, a shivering jerk and the punt flies back, as the gun's report echoes from the hills like thunder across the sea. By now the geese are gone down stream gaggling vociferously and so loudly they can be heard four miles away, but our attention lies ahead. Rowing forward, the shot seems longer than we thought, yet there they are, lying like great baskets set afloat, gently moving with the tide. Soon the last is gathered; it has been a successful shot. It is 1.15 a.m. and the stars are brightly shining, the fog has somewhat cleared, and the river traffic ceased, but the geese are still there calling.

GEESE IN THE GREAT FROST OF '47

By J. Wentworth Day

Normally the inn windows gazed on tidal water, on saltings and the shining vista of the estuary. But on that day in February, 1947, the sea was frozen. The saltings were feet deep in snow. Icebergs, as large as fishing smacks, piled fantastically on the shore.

Outside, the great sailing barge, 'Black Eagle,' creaked at the inn quay. Beyond lay another barge and another, and beyond those towering masts, pointing like icy fingers into the hard blue of the winter sky, lay smack on smack, punt beyond punt, dinghy and skiff, all fast in the ice, shrouded in snow.

So it had gone on for weeks. They said it was the worst winter for fifty years. In places the snow was fifteen feet deep, piled in monumental waves, like frozen Atlantic rollers. One lone smack, lying in Death Creek, whence its two fishermen owners worked their punts night and morning, sent over six hundred brent geese and widgeon to the local game dealer's shop in a fortnight, for the fowl were in thousands–in tens of thousands. By day they moved in black clouds, in long straggling skeins, over the ice and the glittering tide. By night they passed over in a river of wings. It was the winter of which wildfowlers dream. Such clouds of fowl, such wastes of ice and snow, such bitter nights of stars as you see only in steel engravings of our grandfather's days.

"Never seen anything like it," said Alf. "That's the deepest snow and the worst ice I've knowed in me time. And I've been gunnin' on this river forty odd year."

"Ha! You're only a younker," said an earringed old reprobate from the window settle. "Time I was a little owd boy the snow was right up to me bedroom winders. Yew couldn't git out of the door. That was shut fast by the snow, right above the lintel. Me Dad and me Mum and us nippers was held fast in the house for a week. Couldn't git out nor in. We lived on salt hog an' a sack o' spuds. An' when me Mum wanted to bile the kettle, me Dad shoved me out o'the top winder with a bucket to git some snow to fill the kittle. That *wuss* a winter!"

"Liars I've knowed in me time." Remarked Alf casually, looking fixedly out of the window. "Big 'uns, too, in foreign parts. An' yew can *enjoy* their yarns–but–liars I allus run from! Cum on' mates. Let's git gunnin'!"

Out we went, to an icy street where dogs moved stiffly. Fishermen shuffled by with mufflers round their ears. House doors and windows were shut fast. And thence, in a motorcar that rolled like a ship over frozen ruts, we voyaged afield to pick up those three fowlers whom neither snow nor ice can daunt—Lord Lisle, Colonel 'Chutney' Gordon-Dickson, and Major Philip Martin. Now these are three mighty men, proven in the ways of marsh and mudflat.

Five or six miles out of the town we turned left by a farm road, so deep in snow that you could only tell it was a road by the tops of the fences on either side. Cattle marshes stretched in a white prairie. Carrion crows beat the bitter waste like hounds. Woe betide the partridge crouching under the lee of a snow drifted hedge if those cold eyes came near.

We topped the sea wall. Beyond lay the estuary. Three miles wide, void of ships, the near shore a white and broken land of grinding floes, of icebergs and snowdrifts. The far shore was a glimmer of ghostly white—a faint, fantastic land of little white hills crowned by ghostly farmhouses.

In middle distance rose an island, elm crowned and lonely. Great floes of ice, an acre or more in extent, moved solemnly down on the tide. Black masses of duck were sitting on them, riding down river like marooned sailors. Decoy Point ran out into the estuary. On the lee shore, sitting in the sun, were fleets of fowl. I picked them up through the glasses in the cold sunlight. Forty or fifty brent geese strutted in their calm, deliberate way. A big parcel of widgeon were asleep on the mud. Half a dozen pintail sailed, graceful as yachts, on the water. Three herons waded in the shallows. A host of small waders flickered back and forth.

Beyond, five or six huge birds rode at anchor. They looked like Canada geese. Alf had shot one with his punt gun a week earlier, before the punt was locked in the ice. It weighed fifteen pounds. And that was something of an event, for the Canada goose has only begun to visit the Essex flats in the last year or two. Driven south from Norfolk by gales and snow, they may, who knows, before long become a resident goose. And that will be a notable gain to the fauna of our long, indented, lonely coast.

Half an hour passed. The wind came out of the east like a knife. Geese and duck passed up and down river in constant trips and flights. Gradually the flats bared. Weed grown piles stood up, black and glistening. A stranded buoy tipped sideways on the mud, like a gigantic fishing float. We straggled out across the flats, following Alf, ankle deep in frozen mud, and spaced out across a mile of mud where rills of salt water ran like mill races. All the vast flats glittered in the sun. Up river, a great lagoon of salt water, a mile and a half wide and three miles long, was dotted with fowl. Down river the estuary glittered to a far, snow-misty horizon where a great four masted Finnish barque, a timber ship, swung at anchor, spars and rigging gleaming in the sun. It might have been midwinter in the England of three centuries before.

I settled down on a bit of old board, a stranded ice floe at my back, a pile of frozen ice in front. It made a perfect butt. That ring tailed mongrel, Mr. Soapy Sponge, whose heart is of gold, whose mother was a flat-coated retriever, whose father, they say, was a Norfolk harrier, whose cost was thirty shillings, and whose price is above rubies, squatted, flailing snow and mud with a ceaseless tail, searching sea and sky with amber, questing eyes. Not a feather that moves escapes him. No tide nor mud can daunt him. Not a whimper of wings misses his ear. That day he was to set the high peak of all dog endeavour. It is a true tale, worth telling.

Presently the birds began to come. First, seven bar-geese swept by, shining in chestnut and white. I let them go. We do not shoot the gaudy, lovely shelduck, too lovely to be killed, too fishy to be eaten. Yet that winter the fishermen were sending them to London shops at four shilling a bird, and underfed citizens, that year of Socialist promise of plenty, were eating them gladly.

Then, through the glasses, I saw seven Brent geese, coming low over the water, beating along in that deceptive, slow-seeming way of theirs. Raggedly they flew, like great black crows, with pointed wings, seeming to travel at all too easy a pace. And that is where the brent defeats the beginner again and again, for their flight is far faster then it appears. They were coming straight for me. I crouched low behind the piled ice. Behind, in a deep cut, a pool of salt water gurgled. A great block of ice popped suddenly to the surface like a grey backed seal. Soapy turned his head. And that, I think, turned the geese. They swung right handed, passed me across the mud at no more than thirty five yards, flying low. I swung up the double eight bore, which weighs near seventeen pounds and fires five ounces of shot, and let drive.

A thunderous boom, a billow of white smoke, another boom, and I sat back as though a horse had kicked me. Not a goose fell. Clean missed with both barrels at under forty yards. And that, my masters, points the moral that although a heavy gun may give you much greater range, infinitely more penetration and a bigger pattern, it is no gun for quick, close shooting or for low shots.

I let pass a trip of a dozen grey plover, scything low over the water. An easy shot for a game gun but far too fast and close to risk the waste of a four and a quarter inch cartridge from the big gun. Other trips and bunches of waders passed quickly. Redshank flew within fifteen yards. Stints, or ox-birds as we call them in Essex, flashed past, a foot above the mud in shimmering clouds. They turned and wheeled in the winter sunshine like falling silver. Once I heard an oyster catcher, a rare bird on those flats. Yet they bred there forty years ago. What looked like a trip of ruffs and reeves fled past at a distance. Great saddle-backed gulls swung high overhead on slow wings, barking like dogs. They were hunting the slain, on the track of the wounded.

Once a peregrine falcon swished past, not fifteen yards away, beating a bare yard above the ebbing tide. I could see its dark moustache, its yellow tiger eyes and hooked beak perfectly. An easy shot. But why shoot a peregrine for the mere sake of killing a rare bird? There are far too few of them in a world bent on destroying beauty when it finds it. Then, far ahead, a bunch of brent lifted from a mud bank where a red and black can-buoy tipped sideways on the flood. They swung past the end of the island, winging raggedly against a background of spidery elms. They were wide of me. They would pass over Jack Lisle. They did. A double flash, far twin reports. One goose crumpled up its neck and thudded in the mud with a "sock." A second glided forward on bent wings, suddenly doubled up and came down in a shallow, emptying lagoon. Soapy was out of the butt like a flash. He reached the pool, grabbed the goose and came trotting back to my butt and delivered it to hand.

Other geese passed wide. A cock widgeon came over, high as an archangel. James Gordon-Dickson pulled it out of the clouds. Then from behind came a whicker of wings, a hoarse, startled "Cr-onk! Cr-onk!" and dead overhead, nine brent geese, huddled in a startled bunch. I missed with the first barrel, for one sea boot caught on the trailing corner of my oilskin and threw me off balance. The second barrel cut down a goose as they planed away forty yards off. Nothing to be proud of.

As the great gun boomed across the flats, ducks and geese sprang from the water and swept back and forth. Straight towards me were coming seven brent geese. Soapy was plodding across the flats with the dead goose. Would the oncoming birds see him and veer? They came straight on. A hundred yards, necks outstretched, wings beating evenly, all seven in that perfect V which you see so often in pictures and so seldom in actuality. Eighty yards, fifty. I threw up the gun, swung that mass of metal a yard and a half in front of the leader, pulled–"Broomp!" Down he came like a sack of wheat. They bunched suddenly, fled away to windward–I fired again. Down came a second, winged. Soapy was on him like a flash, leaving the dead bird to lie. There was the quick mongrel intelligence.

More shots across the mud from Jack Lisle. A goose toppling headlong. A double shot from Alf and another goose socked into the mud on the far island foreshore. Five pintail and thirty widgeon went over 'Colonel Chutney.' James's long chambered twelve cut one down and sent another away in a long, planing dive, to light, far out in the river, near half a mile away. A great cloud of green plover went over in a fantasia of wings.

Far down the river off Decoy Point, Philip's gun cracked, thin and whip-like–five times running. Through the glasses a great ragged cloud of fowl, geese, ducks and waders, veered back and forth over the point. Seven great birds lumbered up-river on heavy, beating wings. Wild swans or Canada geese? It was too far to see, even with the glasses.

A bunch of widgeon were coming straight for me. Soapy's eyes watched intently. His tail hammered the mud, splashing me from head to foot. Sixty yards up and I let drive. One to the first barrel and a pricked bird to the second; a bird that went wide towards the island and was cut down handsomely by Alf. As neat an eye-wipe as one could wish. And Alf, be it said with praise was shooting with an old, rusty twelve bore whose barrels were so loose that you could see daylight at the breech face. A moment later a solitary brent came past him like the wind, travelling low. He cut it over headlong.

Time passed. The salt pool behind my butt gurgled and whirled. Great floors of ice, stained grey by mud, suddenly caved in. Swirling water alive with snow bubbles hissed and rustled on its under ice journey to the sea. A party of ox-birds lit on the mud not twenty feet in front of the hide and ran about like mice. Odd shots came from right and left. But the main flight was over. It was near low water and, by the sun, two in the afternoon. Lines of geese cronked on distant mudbanks. A cormorant went over like a black crossbow. A heron was fishing in the shallows of Death Creek. Far away, in the main channel, a great white shape, long and low and turreted, moved slowly with the tide. It looked like a frost encrusted gunboat. I slewed the glasses on it. An iceberg, the biggest berg I have ever seen on the Essex coast, an odd, fantastic ship which sailed, manless, out to sea.

Presently Alf came plodding across the mud, gun under one arm, a bunch of mud draggled ducks and geese in the other hand. He picked up Jack Lisle, who sat, crouched like a fox, in a gut in the mud, and the twain joined me.

"Dead low water now." Said Alf. "They on't fly much more now till that turn. Better git back to the car and hev our grub."

Back at the car, in the lee of the sea wall, hot rum and coffee, a pork pie and bread and cheese and onions went their proper way. The wind blew keener. It came out of the east like a knife. It bit nose and ears and seared necks like a whiplash. Snow on the gun barrels crystallised hard, sugar like. The iron latch on a field gate stuck to one's hand when it was touched. It was below zero, freezing harder. Presently the tide turned. We went back to our places. For an hour, for two hours, birds passed to and fro, shots rang out. Some fell, some were missed. I gathered three more geese and lost a fourth, picked up a pair of widgeon and missed more than I should have done.

Then the tide flooded us out. We waded back, loaded with birds, plunging once into a hidden, hurrying rill that nearly topped our high boots. Soapy had to swim for it. Back at the sea wall we retired to the car to get out of the wind and get into the rum. The tide flooded over the flats. Ice floes were grinding along the shore. Between us and the island stretched near three quarters of a mile of running sea. Ten minutes more out on those flats would have meant certain death.

Suddenly a goose came from nowhere over Jack Lisle. He fired. It swung out over the salt water, flying low, suddenly crumpled and pitched dead into the flowing tide. The next moment Soapy was swimming strongly. Whatever the misses and malfeasances of his master, the dog at least was determined to redeem them. The goose was a good two hundred yards out. The tide was flowing at four knots and swinging the bird off shore. The water was thick with floating ice. It was actually two degrees below freezing point.

I watched that dog with my heart in my mouth. Yapping incessantly he cut the tide like a motor boat, that frightful ringtail brandishing above the freezing water. The black yapping head and that ridiculous tail faded behind a floating floe. Would he be seized by sudden cramp, throw up his paws and sink? I got out the glasses. He emerged from the other side of the floe, still swimming strongly. The goose was drifting steadily out two hundred yards from the shore. And the tide was taking dog and bird still further out. High, determined yaps floated shoreward. The glasses followed that gallant little head.

He reached the goose, grabbed it, swung round and started to battle back against the tide-set. I wondered whether the bird would drag his head down, whether icy water would fill and choke his throat–wondered too, if a cramp stricken dog suddenly sank or floated. No need for such fears. Steadily he forged through the tide, the goose held high above the water, that monstrous, unforgivable tail wagging gaily.

He brought the bird, blinded though his eyes were by its heavy body, straight to the water's edge in front of me, wallowed through mud and ice, dropped it at my feet, smiled broadly– and proceeded to roll frantically on a floe. Then he swallowed a mouthful of snow. A hand tapped me on the shoulder. There stood a stranger, thigh booted, head and neck muffled in a great balaclava wool helmet, a heavy ten bore across his oilskin coated shoulder.

"I don't know you sir, but I'd like to raise my hat to your dog," he said quietly. "It's the longest swim I've ever seen in salt water–five hundred yards if it was an inch, and I've never seen a dog before that would even face the water on a day like this. I watched it from the sea wall and it crowned the day for me."

Thus ended Saturday, February 15th, in the winter of 1947, perhaps the coldest day for fifty years, a day that ended with a bag between us of fourteen brent geese gathered, twenty eight ducks in the bag, and a little dog exalted above men.

THE MAGIC OF GOOSE SHOOTING

By G.K. Yeates

The pursuit of the wild goose is proverbial for its difficulties and its disappointments. It is for just that very reason that its followers are the most enthusiastic of all shooting men. They have to be, or they would give it up in disgust. The blasé dilettante is a type unknown amongst wildfowlers, for he is smothered at birth before ever he has graduated even into the junior forms of that hard school.

The fascination of goose shooting needs no advertisement, for it has produced not only a literature but an art of its own, and even among those of us who can pretend to no skill with either pen or brush there are few who have not found in its atmosphere something of the poetic. Perhaps this is the fruit of those wonderful dawns and gorgeous sunsets out of which so often the goose shooter sees his quarry coming in to feed or returning late to their beloved muds. But that cannot be all the story, for there are many dawns and many sunsets which are neither beautiful nor inspiring, but unbelievably uncomfortable and dreary—and it is those unlovely dawns which are from the point of view of the bag the most profitable. Its inspiration, in part, comes from the wideness, the generosity of the horizons against which geese are to be shot.

Today we live so cramped a life, confined by city walls or office desks, that the spirit goes out in full to meet freedom, and on the great mudflats where the geese congregate are space and quietness undreamt of by the town-lubber. The saltings and the ooze are not everybody's idea of a cup of tea, but to those who have come to know them, not only at midday but at dawn and evening and under the soft light of the moon, they are full of beauty, a world in which the sky plays a bigger part than usual in our conceptions of scenery.

Even so, if the poet rises in us as we wait, we owe it to the geese themselves, for under the sun there is nothing wilder. Forget the inspiring spectacle of a straggling skein going inland at dawn; forget that wonderful clamour with which they announce their rising or their settling, or the far-carrying small talk which accompanies them as they journey. Think instead of the great distances they travel and of the remote places in which they live.

Here with us it is the sandbanks and muds of the Solway,

Wash, Humber or Severn, but from those each day they at least visit civilisation, marshes where windmills stand and potato fields where are scattered farmsteads. It is not of the ooze I think when I pick up a dead pink-foot or white-front, but of the place that saw its birth and from which it has journeyed, perhaps many times, to this patch of mud from which I pick it up. Where, pink-foot did you first see the light of day? Was it on a volcanic cliff where Icelandic farmer rarely ventured? Or did your eyes first look out over Spitzbergen's wastes, over bays to islands where your lesser cousins, the brent geese, nest? And you, white-front that now I gather from the saltings' edge, came you from that wilderness of tundra that spreads east and west along the Polar shore from the great delta of Petchora or Yenisei?

Whenever I pick up 'my' goose, such thoughts as these are always mine. One day I hope that I may journey forth and see these Arctic birthplaces for myself. No wonder we think of geese as wild.

How to shoot a grey goose, be it grey-lag, white-front, pink-foot or bean, is a question I would only attempt to answer with the greatest diffidence. As I write, I can almost hear my friends quietly muttering about the proof of the pudding being in the eating and practising what I preach! Yet, omitting such general subjects as the time and hour, weather conditions, gun and ammunition, there are two points worthy of the greatest emphasis.

The first is the ability to keep *still* when a skein is approaching. And by still I mean the type of immobility which Medusa dealt out to her victims. You are not being still if you move your head to follow the skein: you are not being still if you move your feet to get them more advantageously placed to rise and shoot; you are not being still if you have not seen to it that your mackintosh collar or coat-tails do not blow in the wind. *Nothing* about you or on you must move–except your eyes. You can move your eyeballs in their sockets and you may breathe–but that is all. I am frequently astonished at some people's ideas of being still. Their heads turn; they move their hands into position up the barrel of the gun; they even move the gun. And when the skein veers off and passes them by a clear 100 yards, they wonder why! He who can lie dead still on an open sandbank stands a better chance at geese than a jack-in-the-box in the deepest creek bottom.

The second point concerns the time to shoot. If you remain as still as a post, there will come a moment when stillness must be translated into violent and speedy action. Now 'the beak,' the head and neck, is the place to put the charge with every sporting bird, and while I do not believe in these stories of the armour plating of a goose's breast feathers, the 'beak' is with geese more than ever the spot to hit, if only because shots are normally on the long side. But although this is the case, do not on that account take a goose in front of you. An on-coming goose is the most deceptive bird I know. When it looks like a Dornier, it is often 80 to 100 yards away. On the other hand, unless a gale is blowing into the birds, when it will be found advantageous for the second barrel, do not let your goose pass you. The moment to rise and shoot is easy, for it is the moment when the bird is *closest to you*, i.e. directly overhead or to one side. Then move quickly, but you will have plenty of time, even with white-fronts, which can rise in a miraculous manner, to put your charge into the head and neck. As geese are usually high, you will want every yard they will give you. If you rise to them in front, you will merely add yards to a distance that is already straining to your gun.

And lastly, one very serious word in plea for the geese. A goose at 10 yards looks enormous, at 50 it is huge, at 100 it is still a big bird. *Do not take long shots*. I am well aware of the distance at which geese can be killed by magnums and by 8–bores, and I have read gunmaker's claims. But although there may be a chance of success, pause to think of the odds against killing and of the evens on wounding, if only with one or two pellets. I am horrified by the useless 'banging away on chance' that goes on whenever a goose takes the air. Successful long shots are not cause for satisfaction and congratulation, but for reprobation and the stern reading of a lecture on sportsmanship. When in doubt, hold your fire altogether and let the skein go trumpeting undisturbed inland. If in our anxiety to get our goose we are prepared deliberately to wound many of the noblest birds that fly, we would do well to put our guns away for all time and cease to sully the name of good sportsmanship. Geese are not rats, but are among the grandest of all living things. We do well never to forget it.

WILDFOWL SHOOTING FROM "TUBS."

By Major Arthur Hood (1909)

There is no better sport to be enjoyed with the gun in these islands than the pursuit of wild duck–the genuine article, not the hand reared.

It is a great addition to the sporting amenities of any estate to have wildfowl shooting in some form or other as one of the possibilities of amusing your friends in rough or hard weather. Hand reared ducks may fly well and give very good fun, but it is not by any means the same thing as the pursuit of the wild visitors.

The great majority of the wild duck tribe, such as mallard, teal, widgeon, shovellers, gadwell, &c; have their breeding grounds in the far north. They visit this country during the winter months, when frozen out of their more northern breeding grounds. As a rule the best way of circumventing these winter visitors is by flighting, either at day-break or just before dusk.

There are a few favoured places where a large stretch of bog, or marsh lined lake, enables the owner to place 'tubs' or 'hides' at various favourite spots, and give sport to quite a large number of guns throughout the day, such as Lord Castletown's 'Curragh' in Queen's County, Lord Dunleath's bog near Downpatrick, Mr. Hill's shooting at Blagdonlake near Bristol, Colonel Bruce's lake at Ballysullion near Lough Neagh, and some few others.

As regards flighting. In my opinion the early morning flight is the most enjoyable, and it is in one way the most satisfactory, as it is much easier to pick up the results of one's sport after when the flighting is over in the strong light of day; whereas when the evening flight is finished it is often a most hopeless business stumbling about in the dark amongst high rushes and bog-holes of unknown depth, seeking for even the dead birds–not to mention any unfortunate wounded there may be; and disastrous mistakes may occur.

For instance, on one occasion when staying at Pitfour in Aberdeenshire, there had been a full gale with driving rain all day which had kept us to the house. Late in the afternoon our host suggested that it might be a good evening to get in the line of flight from the lake, which is close to the house and not far from the sea. This lake is never disturbed, and becomes the winter home of many hundreds of wild duck and widgeons and other rarer specimens of the duck tribe, who seem to appreciate this immunity, and allow an observer to approach quite close to them. But at dusk, when they take flight to their feeding grounds in the marshes and neighbouring streams, very good sport may be had if one can only hit off their line.

On the occasion I am thinking of I took up a position behind an old oak tree in the park, about a quarter of a mile away from the lake, and had capital sport until it became too dark to see to shoot. The next business was to pick up the slain, of which there were about a dozen (a difficult job without a retriever). Having searched all over the place–there were still two missing of the required number–I was just giving it up as a bad job, when I almost stepped on a duck in the dark, who started off waddling and fluttering to the lake. After a most exciting pursuit the fugitive was caught and knocked on the head. On returning towards the oak tree another flutterer was stumbled upon, who gave even more trouble to catch than the previous one; however, he was duly captured, put out of his misery, and I returned in triumph to the house with the full number and took them round to the game larder.

On looking them over by lamp light, imagine my horror on discovering that the two wounded birds that had been so skilfully run down in the dark were two very choice pinioned specimens of a certain call-duck which my host had recently turned out on the lake, and were the apple of his eye. The poor birds had evidently wandered up to the oak tree in search of any belated acorns they might find.

As my host was not at this time enjoying the best of health, I thought it wiser, of course entirely on *his* account that the specimens should be immediately plucked by one of the ladies of the kitchen before he examined them on the following morning. This was accordingly carried out, and I don't think the circumstance has ever been mentioned to him. If by any chance this little story should meet his eye, I trust that the statute of limitations will prevail on his well known kindness of heart, and that he will forgive this deplorable accident, which occurred some twenty years ago.

To return to the subject of early morning flighting, it is advisable to make one's preparations in daylight on the previous afternoon, and having selected the exact spot you wish to occupy the following morning, to put up marks to enable you to find your way in the dark. If the spot selected should happen to be in water, it will be far better to leave the retriever behind, with instructions to have him brought to you when the shooting is over. For even the boldest and hardiest dog suffers terribly from standing long in ice cold water, and it is not fair to tax his future health in this way, if it can possibly be avoided.

The higher the wind the better the sport, as the ducks will fly lower and the sound of firing will not be heard so distinctly. Having taken up position behind some bush or screen of reeds in the spot selected, and whilst waiting for the first pale glimmer of dawn in the eastern sky, watching the twinkling stars gradually fade and disappear before the majestic appearance of their more brilliant arrival, the sun, it is interesting to note how very much alive this apparently sleeping marsh really is.

The whistle of an otter close at hand is answered by another on the far side of the river, the hoarse croak of the baldheaded coots is almost continuous, the splutter of a moorhen as she flies across some neighbouring pool, the mournful cry of the curlew as he makes his way from his inland feeding place to a certain sand spit he knows of on which to pass the day. Or perhaps the honk-honk of a gaggle of wild geese also on their way to the sea and safety, or a curious wheezy sound which means that Mr. Woodcock, gorged with worms from an aldermanic repast, is heavily winging his way back to a nice, warm, dry nook beneath a holly bush which he has frequented for the last two winters for ruminating and digestive purposes—all these varied sounds are apt to distract one's attention from the immediate object of this early morning visit, when all at once a faint whistling of wings overhead, accompanied by a low quacking chuckle, announces the earliest arrival of the wild ducks we are especially awaiting.

It is still so dark that it is impossible to see these first arrivals, who settle in a pool amongst the rushes only a few yards away, and we strain our eyes in a vain attempt to distiguish their exact whereabouts; it is quite certain that they are within a few yards, as we can hear their splashing and chuckles of satisfaction. As the light improves it is just possible to distinguish the ghostly forms of duck, widgeon and teal as they dash past overhead. When the bird is visible in this light he is certain to be within killing distance. How satisfactory is the splash or thud amongst the rushes that tells of a successful shot!

It is wonderful how all the duck tribe, especially teal, when suddenly surprised by a shot in this faint light, seem to instantaneously check the forward motion of their flight, no matter how fast they may be coming, and mount straight into the air, disappearing into the overhead darkness seemingly without effort. As the light grows stronger the arrivals become fewer and fewer, until it is not worth waiting any longer. Having signalled for the retriever, the work of picking up can be carried on under the most favourable conditions.

Flighting wild geese is even more exciting–the uncertainty is so great as to whether they will come within shot or not; a moonlight night combined with a gale of wind and snow on the ground is the best time for this. Geese are extraordinarily regular in their movements. A friend once told me that there is a certain island of his Norwegian salmon river at which the geese used to arrive year after year on the same date and almost exactly at the same hour from their Siberian nesting grounds. In fact, as he said, "You could almost set your watch by them."

One year, being unexpectedly recalled to England, he happened to be passing the island in the little coastal steamer on the very day the geese usually arrived. He remarked this to the captain, and that it was just about the right hour for them to appear. A few moments afterwards the captain said, "There they are, Sir"–and away to the north a little gaggle was seen slowly making for the island–the advance guard of the northern invaders.

It is said that the geese begin their migration across the tundra of Northern Siberia before their wing feathers are sufficiently developed for flight; that they march across the flat country, swimming any rivers, until at length they can take to flight; and that the earliest arrivals are nearly always young birds of the first hatch.

When quartered in Ireland some years ago, two brother officers and myself took some shooting on the banks of the Shannon. There were a good many geese about, and our tame 'bog trotter' reported that three flocks passed over a certain bush on the river bank as punctually as possible each morning at nine o'clock, on their way to other feeding grounds on the far side.

Chancing to be down there alone on one occasion, I determined to test the accuracy of his information. The first morning, having arrived within 100 yards of the bush a minute or two late, sure enough the geese were coming on in battalions. As I was completely in the open, and the day being calm, they were flying high; the only thing to do was to lie flat on my back, hoping they would not notice me. This was successful. The next morning was one of those red letter days which one looks back to with great satisfaction.

Struggling out in the teeth of a gale shortly before daybreak to a sort of backwater of the main river, which we had fed with maize for some days, and which certain ducks had already discovered, I had a very good three quarters of an hour's flighting, getting 12 heavy duck, as they call mallards in Ireland. Then back to breakfast and a sharp walk of something over a mile, arriving at the bush in good time, armed with a double barrelled 8-bore.

At almost exactly nine o'clock there was a tremendous clamour on the red bog beyond the fir trees to the left front, and immediately afterwards the first V-shaped 'gaggle' came slowly beating up wind and flying low straight for my hide. Two were secured out of this lot. The next gaggle evidently saw the commotion occuring in the ranks of their predecessors, and, slightly deflecting their course, passed out of range; but the last flock came straight over the bush, one being killed, whilst another, hard hit, managed to get to the river.

Shortly afterwards the 'bog-trotter' arrived in a canoe from the shooting lodge, bringing with him my 12 bore. After searching in vain for the wounded goose, he took the 8-bore and the three geese home, whilst I returned overland through the red bog, killing six woodcocks and one snipe, and arriving just in time to catch the mid-day train back to Dublin.

Perhaps the best morning's flighting I ever enjoyed was

obtained last winter, 1909, at Longparish on the Test, now in the occupation of Mr. Diggle. This place was formerly the home of the great Col Hawker, who has left a diary of the great things he did here in the early part of the 19th century with rod and gun—indeed, according to his account he seems hardly ever to have missed anything he shot at! One of Mr. Diggles guests, Mr. H. Noble, went out for the early morning flight, and returned to breakfast with upwards of 70 wild duck, in addition to seven or eight teal to his own gun. A truly red letter morning.

The evening flight is very much the same sort of sport, plus the before-mentioned difficulties of picking up. The time the ducks begin to come is, as a rule, just when the lighthouses are lit up or the candles appear in the cottager' windows.

Some capital days have been enjoyed in tubs or from behind hides on large bogs and lakes. At Lord Castletown's place, Granston, in Queen's County, there is a vast stretch of marsh some six or seven miles long by perhaps a mile wide. It is so wet and intersected by small rivers that it is difficult to walk, and for the same reason difficult to poach (the curse of most estates in Ireland). This bog is jealously looked after by a fine specimen of the Irish marsh-keeper, Boyce by name, who knows every inch of it. Any poacher who dared show his nose on his domain would be certain to receive a very warm reception.

Several large tubs have been sunk in various spots known to be favoured by the ducks. Success on these occasions depends almost entirely on the wind; the higher it is the better, and it depends on the direction of the wind which particular tubs and hides are used. Before starting, watches are compared and lots drawn for the particular tubs selected for occupation. Everyone is warned not to shoot before a certain hour, by which time each gun should have arrived at his allotted stand. It is a fine sight to see the disturbance created by the firing of the first shot—many hundreds of duck, teal, widgeon, shovellers, plover, snipe, etc. will be seen flying about in all directions.

When shooting from a tub, as the quarters are rather confined, it is very difficult, especially for a big man, to turn quickly. It is therefore best to make up one's mind to keep a lookout in one direction only, and that downwind; to keep as still as possible, and not to shoot until the result ought to be a certainty. Unless a bird is killed quite dead the chances are it will never be recovered, even if the keeper has the help of a good retriever, as these wounded birds have the knack of creeping and diving until they reach one of the numerous streams that intersect the marsh in all directions, eventually falling a prey to gigantic pike or rats.

Many otherwise experienced shots waste no end of cartridges by shooting at duck at impossible distances, in the hope of bringing off a lucky coup, but there is little satisfaction to be gained by doing this, and much unnecessary misery and suffering is inflicted on the unfortunate birds.

A piece of chalk in the pocket is a great help, as one can put a mark on the inside of the tub showing the direction in which the bird has fallen, and by having different lengths of mark to represent under 20 yards, between 20 and 40, and over that distance. It will greatly assist the memory later on when the keeper arrives in the punt.

Very good mixed bags have been made on this, Curragh, and also on Lord Dunleath's further north in County Down. This bog, lying close to the town of Downpatrick, and not far from the sea, is the winter home of great quantities of duck and teal. A great deal depends on the state of the tide here, if it is high and the sea rough, both duck and teal speedily return to the bog if they cannot find smooth water outside. At Ballyscullion, Colonel Bruce has run out a line of tubs into a long narrow lake a few miles below Lough Neagh. By sending a boat to disturb the ducks at either end, good sport may be had here for an hour or so, after which they leave for the larger and safer waters of the Great Lough.

At Blagdon, near Bristol, it is a case of a large artificial lake some three miles long by nearly a mile wide—hides and tubs have been placed along the shore at certain favourable points. On one occasion I think upwards of 250 wildfowl were bagged here in one day by Mr. Hill and his friends.

A SOLWAY FOWLER

By E. Blezard

The hazardous pursuit of wildfowling has produced a race of men known all along our seaboard for their hardihood, outdoor craft and, in spite of the attendant dangers of their calling, longevity.

Now their period seems to be drawing to a close, particularly on the Cumberland Solway where once flourished a most notable band. Here they were wildfowlers and more; as skilled in the use of the haaf-net, that huge hand net for salmon, peculiar to the Solway, as in the use of a fowling piece or in the handling of a gunning punt. More than ordinarily keen observers they were as well, in some instances valuable recorders, and all of them came to rank as grand old worthies, being without exception each one of them an outstanding personality.

One of the last of these almost vanished veterans was James Storey, of Anthorn, who died in June 1946, after passing his eighth decade. Jim Storey, as he was spoken of in wide

178

friendship and regard, and by which name he was known far even beyond the bounds of his native Cumberland, not only wrested a hard living from the Solway but also found happiness in the doing of it.

His cottage, similar to those of the other men of his pursuits, was not far removed from the tideway and was characterised by a tidy and well tilled garden, reflecting that love of order common in those people who live close to Nature. Inside, other than a gun rack and a case containing a couple of prized dotterel, there was little to distinguish the cottage from that of any other Cumbrian villager. That gun rack, the gift of a woodworker who at times came to try his luck at shooting on the marshes, has held besides Jim's two or three guns, those of amateur wildfowlers from all parts of the kingdom.

Outside, of course, on land or water, as ruled by circumstances, lay the decked in, Solway built punt in its white paint to betoken the whereabouts of Jim's home. Between seasons, the 'big' gun, from which many and many pounds of lead had each been driven by four ounces of blasting powder, rested in a shed with its muzzle carefully plugged and its breech covered in an oil wrapping.

Jim certainly maintained all the vigour and zest of his fellow fowlers and often enough on winter days was out in his gunning punt after widgeon or other fowl when most men of his years had long been content with the neighbourhood of the fireside. In his seventies he regularly tramped a good many rough miles daily to and from his fluke nets, oft times setting out before the dawn, according to the ebb of the tide, and it was towards the end of his activity that he gathered some thirty widgeon into his punt after a well placed shot made not far from his own doorway.

In the season that the first all white plumaged barnacle goose appeared on the Solway, Jim unsuccessfully tried for it with his shoulder gun, with which, by the way, and as in the case of many other countrymen, he was one of those high performers who go down unrecorded. One day, by chance, he found himself squinting along his punt gun at this white barnacle and—well, he pulled. It was just one of those occasions when the gun misfired, but whether it was also one of those on which he slackened a tooth or two he did not say!

By habitually firing while holding the lanyard between his jaws and jerking back his head, while his hands were oversides to steady the punt, Jim had had his ivories considerably reduced in number by the kick of the gun. Latterly, he discovered that a piece of old motor car inner tube on the end of the lanyard was not so hard on the teeth.

Very wise as to the ways of the wild life around him, and to the vagaries of the Solway, its weather and its tides, he invariably knew where grey geese or barnacle geese, or mallard or other duck were to be found and just why they would be in that particular place. His trick of glancing around the sky and unerringly forecasting the day's weather was an almost uncanny one. If Jim advised you to take a waterproof when you were leaving his front gate for the marshes, then you would find that you would need that waterproof before the end of the day.

Like many more shooting men, Jim carried about with him a selection of pellets from an ill directed charge. These were lodged in the thick of his leg, and on occasion he would half humorously make a pronouncement on the weather according to just how they were making themselves felt. They were as reliable as the 'rheumatics' by which old country folk are wont to swear.

Many students of nature, eminent ornithologists among them, from all parts of the British Isles, have foregathered in Jim's cottage during the long years that he lived at Anthorn. Much they learned under his guidance, as, for instance, the habits of nesting dunlin on the salt marshes, and much more from his wealth of experience. His prefatory, 'I mind once . . . . . .' often enough led to a modest account of bird happenings which, to his visitors, would have been among the thrills of a lifetime. His deep interest in the ways of birds and his quickness to note the occurrence of an uncommon or rare visitor, whether duck, wader, gull or skua, are evidenced in local literature. Generosity in imparting his accumulated knowledge was one of his great characteristics, as was a ready kindliness in bestowing any material gift within his power.

Although many of those visitors who derived so much pleasure and interest from calling on Jim did not attain to anywhere near his number of years, there are still many more to remember him. Among those to whom he remains a fine memory there is a realisation that though picturesque cottages still stand, and wildfowl still come and go, a place without an affectionately regarded inhabitant is an almost empty place. Such is Anthorn to them, without Jim Storey.

FALKLAND ISLAND GEESE

By 'Kelper'

The stalking and outwitting of geese is a sport that is enjoyed in all parts of the world. The particular goose shoot of which I write took place some eight thousand miles away in the Falkland Islands which lie in the South Atlantic Ocean off the South American coast.

I had just returned to the Falklands from a spell of duty at a base in the Antarctic, to the comparative hurly-burly of life in Port Stanley, the only town in the Falklands, with its dances in the gym, mail every six weeks or so, and several good hostelries, including the most southerly 'pub' in the British Empire. Here firearm certificates are issued for the asking, without the usual 'argy-bargy' encountered in England. Here also it is cheaper to drink whisky than beer and cigarettes are extremely inexpensive.

One afternoon in the middle of winter, about July, I took a walk across the camp ("camp" is a word which is derived from the Spanish "campus" which means the countryside or outback) armed with a .22 rifle, on the lookout for a hare of which there were quite a number about.

The camp is covered with grass and diddle-dee bushes which attain a height of about a foot only and which bow to the prevailing wind. There are also patches of balsum-bog which are shiny green growths of vegetation. In the winter there are extensive marshy patches that hold quite a number of snipe and where marsh starlings, which in the Falklands are called robins because they have a brilliant red breast, may be seen. The undersoil is composed almost entirely of peat, often to a depth of many feet. This is the only fuel in the Falklands.

The hares which I was looking for did not seem to be at home that particular afternoon. I had walked several miles without seeing one. Reaching the top of a ridge, I got a view of one of the large ponds that are to be found around the coast of the islands. This one was about a mile away and known as Mile Pond as it is a good mile in length. On it could be seen four white dots which I took at first to be Dominican gulls. On nearer approach I could see that they were geese.

There are three types of goose common in the Falklands. These are the Kelp geese, found only on the seashore, Brent geese, and Upland geese. The two last named are not protected.

The four which were on the pond were Upland geese. I decided to make a stalk. I made a long detour to come up on the other side of the pond by way of the beach which was strewn with large pebbles the size of footballs and over which the going was rough. I had a look over a bank. The geese were still there but at a distance of about a hundred yards and as I am no William Tell I decided that I should have to get closer. There was no cover behind which I could approach so I made my way back to the beach and moved a bit farther down to where there were some diddle-dee bushes. I almost tripped over a seal which was hauled out on the beach sleeping off a meal of cuttlefish.

I was now about sixty yards from the geese and there was quite a bit of cover. The geese were much nearer to the side of the pond and one, which had been out on to the bank, was in the act of returning to the water.

I had a wet crawl on my stomach and finally arrived behind a very small bush about forty yards from my quarry, which were now showing some signs of alarm and beginning to move away. I took careful aim at the neck of the nearest, pressed the trigger, and was pleasantly surprised to see only three birds leave the water. Reloading as quickly as possible to finish off my goose, I was amazed to see a second plunge into the centre of the pond without a flap. The bird that I had fired at was dead also and was being blown into the bank by a good stiff wind. The second one was also drifting in with one wing sticking up into the air as a sail.

I waited until this bird had been blown into the bank and then returned to the spot where I had seen the seal. It had disappeared. By the time I had returned to the pond the goose had almost reached the bank but had grounded about five yards out so I set to work to build a path of stepping stones. This took about half an hour and it was now getting dark. Finally I reached the goose and got back to *terra firma* (or as firm as a peat bog ever is in the winter) and, tying the two birds together by the feet, slung them over my shoulder, one down the front and the other down the back and, with my rifle in my free hand, set off for town.

I can hear the hardy types saying "Why not just have waded in?" A pair of wet feet are to be avoided at all cost in a temperature near freezing and with four or five miles to walk. By the time I had reached the ridge from which I had first seen the geese it was dark and I had to pick my way across some very soft going. Fortunately I could see the light from one of the houses near Port Stanley and this became my guiding star. At my digs I was pleased to get rid of my load of about fourteen pounds of goose and to get my feet in front of the stove.

There was not a mark on the second goose. It was not until it had been plucked that we were able to see what had happened. There was a small nick in the spinal column, which must have been made by the bullet emerging from the first goose. The bullet must have changed its direction slightly by ricocheting off the neck bones. Which goes to show that there is no telling where a spent bullet will go.

Both birds were ganders and young ones at that. This could be seen from the fact that the 'corns' at the wing joints were not very large. The ganders fight in the mating season by flying at each other, pecking, and using their wings as flails. This causes the corns on the wing joints. Old birds of many seasons often have corns almost a quarter of an inch long, are as tough as old boot leather, and not much good for the pot. My two were eaten with due ceremony and appreciation.

IT COULD HAPPEN TO YOU

By Bill Powell

"Drowned by misadventure". From time to time, happily rarely, this headline appears in a newspaper above the account of some wildfowler who has come to an untimely end on the marshes. With the arrogance of youth, and with the confidence of experience and advancing years, the thought occurs "That could never happen to me." But it could, you know—and to you, too!

The three main dangers that can befall the unwary, and even at times the wary, are those of tide, quicksand and of getting lost. It is surprisingly easy to lose oneself on a marsh on a dark night, and still easier in fog. This danger is greatly minimised if you purchase an ordinary map of the district, and before venturing out upon a new marsh, study it in detail. Memorise the local geography landmarks and above all those parts that are tidal. Note the compass bearing that should be followed to regain the mainland. NEVER set foot on a tidal marsh without a compass and a torch with which to read it in the darkness. NEVER fail to find out the height and time of high water. With this knowledge and equipment no one should get into serious trouble.

But suppose you are Mr. Haphazard and suddenly find yourself compassless and completely ignorant of your whereabouts one dark night. What can you do? At first sight the obvious solution is to make for some light, should one be visible, but this may prove a snare and a delusion, for there may be deep water between you and that light. The better plan is to wander around until you find a creek. Creeks invariably drain towards the sea, so that provided the tide is not making, one has only to be followed upstream to lead away from danger. If the tide is making, you should walk in the direction of the flow, but if you have no idea of the state of the tide then study the water for a moment. An incoming tide fills a creek fairly rapidly and brings scum floating on the water. If there is no scum and the water is not rising, you can be fairly confident that the tide is on the ebb.

Suppose the creek fizzles out as so many creeks do, or that one cannot be found. It is then that the stars, if visible, should be used. While a knowledge of astronomy is helpful, it is by no means essential. You will know how deep on to the marsh you originally penetrated. Let us suppose it was half a mile. Select any prominent star and walk about a thousand paces towards it. Within this distance you may either reach the mainland or the outer boundary of the marsh, which may be mudflats or possibly water. Turn your back on the outer boundary and selecting another star, walk until you reach safety.

If on your first walk you reach neither inside nor outside of the marsh the probability is that you are walking parallel to the mainland, in which case you should turn at right angles and walk towards another star until a boundary is reached. Should you reach a fence, then remember the majority of these run from mainland to shore.

With no stars visible the wind should be used. Walk directly into the wind for a thousand paces and if no landmark or creek is reached, turn at right angles again, keeping the wind on, say, your right cheek and see what turns up. It is extremely unlikely that all three of these methods will fail.

The creeks can be used in fog, but of course there are no stars to guide you. If you venture out in fog on a strange marsh, and without a compass, you are past praying for! Should fog threaten, you should make tracks for safety at once. Should you be able to locate the position of the sun, a bearing may be obtained by use of your watch. Point the hour hand towards the sun. A line midway between the hour hand and the "12" on your watch dial will indicate south–always assuming that you have remembered to wind your watch!

Being cut off by the tide is always disconcerting and can be serious. The most important thing is to keep your head and not panic. You must make up your mind whether you are going to stand it out, or make tracks for dry land. If you know, as you should, the time of high water, you can calculate how much higher the water is likely to rise. It is difficult to generalise, as circumstances vary, but it is usually safer to stand still. With luck you won't even get your boots filled. But if you know nothing of the tide times, it is perhaps safer to get moving. If there are cattle on the marsh, make for them for they seem instinctively to know the highest spots of land and, abnormal circumstances apart, seldom drown.

Try to find a long stick, and prod with it to locate holes as you wade. Submerged creeks can usually be spotted by the flow of the water. Beware of tufts in the water, as these may be merely pieces of floating grass. Prod them with your stick before stepping on them. If the worst comes to the worst and you have to swim for it, do not adopt half measures. Stick your gun barrels firmly into the ground for easier location later, remove your waders, coat and any cumbersome clothing, tie them to your gun and make a bee-line for the shore. With luck you will only have to swim for short distances.

Quicksands are usually more alarming than dangerous provided prompt action is taken. By far the most dangerous of quicksand's is the 'bladder' type. This is formed by a skin of turf or sand 'floating' on water. Once the crust is penetrated one is liable to sink like a stone. These can easily be detected, as they 'bounce', and give the impression of walking on jelly. Should you meet one do a very prompt about turn!

The other type consists of soft, semi liquid mud. Directly you suspect that you are in one of these, do not delay to make sure, but lie down flat on your back at once. With your weight thus distributed over a maximum area it is possible to float indefinitely, and by using a kind of swimming back stoke from the elbows, to regain firm ground without serious difficulty. Every second's delay causes you to sink deeper into the mud and makes extrication the more difficult.

Additional buoyancy may be gained by removing your coat and outer clothes and laying these beneath your shoulders. Your gun laid over an oilskin is a great help in gaining purchase with your elbows. Should your legs be firmly embedded it is usually an easy matter to jettison your waders by wriggling out of them. For this reason I never care for waders that strap or lace at the foot.

If you should find somebody badly bogged down it is of little avail to go in after him. Using you as a fulcrum he will merely get you badly stuck as well. Throw him your bag and your coat to put under him. If there is time, run for help, bringing back a rope and some straw or a ladder with which to lay a trail out to him. If he lies flat and keeps still he will not sink. Ineffectual wriggling merely 'puddles' one deeper into the mire.

Of course the best way of dealing with these problems is not to get into these distressing predicaments. Don't be a Mr. Haphazard and venture out ill equipped and alone on strange ground. Remember that by getting into danger yourself you may involve others in considerable trouble, and possibly danger too, when endeavoring to rescue you.

A SUIT OF SACKING FOR LYING IN DUCKHOLES.

FIRST MORNING FLIGHT

By Bill Powell

The electric light was shining in my eyes and I became aware of someone standing by my bed shaking my arm, and of a voice saying "Come on, wake up. It's a great morning for the job."

As a rule I am no lie-a-bed, but last night inroads had been made on both midnight oil and the decanter as we had sat up talking over old times. It was five years since Jim had inherited a little money, resigned his commission, and settled down in a small house on the coast of southern Scotland, and I had not seen him since. On leave from abroad, I had got in touch with him and been invited for a few days wildfowling, about the only form of shooting I had never tried, and one that I regarded with some misgivings.

"It may be great morning for wildfowling (I reflected) but it's not much good for anything else." The wind howled round the eaves and the rain spluttered at the window as I hastily pulled on all the warm clothes that I could muster. Jim had already made a pot of tea when I joined him downstairs, and the tot of rum with which he had laced my cup made life take a slightly less gloomy aspect.

After a five mile drive through the deluge we set off from the car with Jim's Irish water spaniel "Shovvy"–short for Shoveller–close at heel. (All Jim's dogs were named after ducks). Through the inky darkness–"no torches" had been the order–I stumbled across the unfamiliar marsh until we came to the wet sands. Suddenly I was translated into "Page" to Jim's "King Wenceslas", as his footmarks remained outlined in phosphorescent fire for me to follow; not an unusual phenomenon apparently, but to me an eerie experience on that storm washed waste. I could have wished that the promised heat was more apparent! We came to a stretch of water where Jim paused.

"We've got to cross this river," he whispered. "Follow exactly behind me, and when it gets deep move your legs slowly so that you do not swish water over the tops of your thigh boots."

In some trepidation I followed him. The river bottom was muddy and my feet sank into it. Visions of being engulfed in quicksands loomed, and I hoped that Jim knew what he was doing. However, the crossing was made without disaster, and in about half a mile we came to a creek which we followed to its mouth. It was by now a shade lighter and the rain was easing up. I could see that we had reached a hide which had been prepared. The creek formed the back of this, and a semi-circular wall of turves had been built to form cover at the front. Jim had replaced one or two sods which the tide had knocked down, and told me to get myself into it.

"When it gets light, with any luck you'll see geese out there on the flats," he whispered, indicating the direction with a vague sweep of his arm. "If they are there don't fire at any duck that may come over lest you scare the geese away."

With these words he vanished into the gloom while I made myself as comfortable as possible in my extremely damp hide. Less than a week previously I had been in the tropics, and the cold, to me, was intense. The rain ceased and a streak of pale grey appeared in the east. A break came in the clouds through which a patch of shimmering green shone, growing in intensity and size. This was reflected in the vast expanse of wet sands, and entranced with the beauty of my surroundings I forgot the cold and discomfort.

Leaning forward I peered through a small gap to take stock,

and caught my breath, for there, two hundred yards away in the direction Jim had indicated, were some forty geese. They looked enormous, their reflections in the wet sand exaggerating their true size. Most of them were squatting, some apparently asleep. Three were standing upright, motionless, with heads upraised as though listening. One or two were strutting about and occasionally one would stretch upright and flap its great wings. Stealthily I took my field glasses from their case.

As it grew lighter the geese became more active. All were now on their feet and there was much wing flapping and scurrying about. One quarrelsome bird kept lowering its head and charging some goose that apparently had incurred its displeasure. No sound could be heard for the strong wind was blowing towards them. Putting my glasses aside, I broke my gun to re-check that it was loaded. With frozen right thumb I eased the safety catch backwards and forwards. There must be no hitch!

As though at a command the geese all set off walking towards me! I shivered, but with excitement not the cold. After a short distance they stopped their orderly march and commenced a curious ritual. With necks outstretched before them and lowered almost to ground level, they started to sway from side to side, slowly at first, but with rapidly increasing scythe like swings. Then altogether, with a roar of wings clearly audible despite the wind, they rose and headed straight for me. I held my breath, trembling with excitement. This was more wonderful than anything I had envisaged. Rapidly gaining height they flew towards me and I tried to recall Jim's advice.

"Concentrate on the head, and imagine that it is a snipe. Forget the rest of the bird, and give plenty of lead."

Selecting the third bird in the skein, a monster, I tried to concentrate on its head, although the skein looked to me like a flight of bombers coming over. I had never before fired from a sitting position but there was no time to move, so, giving plenty of lead, I let drive. To my great delight I saw my bird crumple up and plummet down to earth, and a feeling of triumph surged through me. It was not until the whole skein had passed overhead that I realized that I had not fired my second barrel!

Although certain that the bird was dead, I could not resist nipping out of my hide to gather it. Once back, I sat stretching out its huge wings and admiring its plumage, when I heard a wild chorus of sound. Hastily discarding my goose and grabbing my gun, I looked out and saw an immense skein flying away to my left. As I looked one folded up and fell earthwards while the rest towered skywards. A shot rang out. Another followed and I saw a goose break formation, turn back, and glide out towards the flats. Some four hundred yards out it made an untidy landing but, making a rapid recovery, waddled off with all speed in the direction of the river. Looking across to where I gathered Jim must be, I saw Shovvy streaking off towards the goose which, however, made the water and started to swim rapidly away. Shovvy bounded in after it and swam in hot pursuit. As she gained on the bird, the goose flapped its wings in desperate endeavour to escape, but the pursuit was relentless. Of Jim there was no sign, so I kept well down in my hide.

Through my glasses I watched the dog catch up with the goose, and after a brief struggle get a hold to her satisfaction and turn for the shore. Progress was slow but at length she gained foothold and walked ashore with her burden. One on dry land she put the bird down to get a more secure hold, and set off to return to Jim.

Another huge skein, followed by several smaller ones, appeared from far out on the tideline, but seeing the dog they were suspicious and veered off. Shovvy put down her burden once or twice to rest, and as the goose did not move, I thought that it must be dead, but such was far from the case. Jim's shot had just cracked the wing tip joint, and the dog brought the bird in unmarked. Eventually the wing tip responded to Jim's amateur bone setting and the goose joined his fine collection of wildfowl on the rough hillside behind his house.

By this time the wind had dispersed much of the cloud and the sun came bounding up as though arising from the depths of the sea, flooding the flats with a brilliance almost painful to behold. In many ways the spectacle seemed unreal. It was more like some stage set in which the artist had allowed his imagination to run riot. The skies were a riot of colour– yellows, bronzes, greens, reds in every variation of hue. The green of the marshes behind was far too vivid to be true, and the snow capped hills to the right with glistening patches of granite on the lower reaches, looking theatrical to a degree. Even the cattle grazing half a mile distant seemed unreal.

So lost was I in my reverie, drinking in the beauty of it all, that when Jim came silently across the close cropped sward from behind me and spoke, he made me start. "I'm desperately sorry," he said, "I'm afraid Shovvy ruined the whole flight prancing about after my runner. But if I hadn't sent her out right away we'd have lost it, and I loathe leaving a wounded bird."

"Ruined the flight?" I replied in amazement, rising a bit stiffly to my feet. "My dear chap, it could not have been more wonderful. Thanks for putting me in such a wonderful spot. How on earth did you know the geese would come over me?"

Jim laughed. "Oh, that," he dismissed his remarkable achievement as of no account. "A bit of luck, that way. One can never know what geese are going to do, but after years of watching 'em you can weigh up the probabilities with a set condition of weather, wind, and tide. Then as often as not they go and do something quite different. We were lucky this morning and might have made a good bag if I hadn't gone and messed things up. I'm so sorry."

"Good heavens, man," I replied, "this flight exceeded my wildest expectations. I'd heard so much about 'wildgoosechasing' that I never really expected to see any, let alone shoot one. When I saw mine fall I was so astonished that I completely forgot my second barrel!"

"You're not the first man to do that with his first goose," Jim grinned. "Come on. I don't know about you, but I could do with some breakfast."

And so home to breakfast, which I attacked with an appetite the like of which I had not had since boyhood. My first flight was over, but it is one that I shall remember to the end of my days.

FIRST RIGHT AND LEFT

By C.T. Hodgkinson

There was snow at Fakenham, not deep, but sufficient to make the motorist exercise extra care; as we approached the coast it diminished. The hamlet of Egmere was clear and at the Golden Gates–the East Lodge to Holkham Park–many pheasants had congregated in the corner of a stubble field for their evening meal.

What a picture they made . . . . . . the more docile looking hens predominating, the full plumaged males, several of which were standing erect on the old stone capped boundary wall, preparatory to their flight to roost in the oaks and conifers which grace the adjoining park and woodlands. One mile to go, 72 miles behind and our journey would be completed, for our rendezvous was the Crown Hotel on the Buttlands at Wells-next-the-sea.

After the process of unloading guns and other shooting impedimenta, Judy, my Springer spaniel, fed and housed, we had tea in front of a welcome log fire. Then, before the evening meal, a walk through narrow Staithe Street towards the old fashioned quay and on to a nearby cottage of weathered red brick with pantile roof, one of several such which had been humble habitations since pre-Victorian days.

We knocked at the weather worn door of the cottage and pressing the Norfolk latch, opened it but inches—it was well nigh impossible to do more, for its progress was arrested by a volume of clothing hanging upon the large protruding nail on the inner side. . . . . oilskins, sou'westers and wildfowler's gear.

"Are you at home, Percy?"

"No," replied a feminine voice, "He say he be a goin' down to his boat."

So down to the water's edge, some eighty yards away, we strolled; it was an early moon, and by its faint power of illumination we could see our pilot busily making secure the anchor of his slender Admiralty- grey painted punt. After greetings we walked towards his cottage; then had a chat on the road outside as to the prospects of the following day, and left Percy, having arranged an early morning tryst for 6.15. Back at the hotel, we spent an after dinner hour in the Oak

Room–a favourite meeting place of wildfowlers–talking over shots missed, opportunities permitted to escape, other disappointments, and by no means least, the pleasurable, and possibly the most vivid, memories of all–when the odd chance in a hundred comes off. Such is the fascination of wildfowling.

Next morning, the church clock was striking six, as, after a cup of tea, some chunks of buttered bread well jammed and hurriedly consumed, we were switching off the lights preparatory to leaving behind the comforts and shelter of a well managed hotel. On the quay we met our pilot. The boat was ready, and soon we were afloat making our way down the main creek, just able to discern the reflection of starlight on the wet grey mud which bordered it. The wind was slight, the morning air frosty and the prospects not very good; but then you don't shoot geese lying in bed–not, at least, unless you are favoured with exceptionally pleasant dreams!

The slow monotonous dip, dip, of the oars. . . . one rowlock creaked with each pull. . . . our eyes became more accustomed to the early morning light, but we could not see any of the bird life which was all around us; here a curlew's call, followed almost immediately by the shrill note of several redshank as disturbed, they hurriedly take their departure to quieter areas of the marsh, awakening others of their kind en route.

At last, chilled to the marrow, we received instructions to alight. Unfortunately for me this was slightly premature and my right thigh boot took in an appreciable quantity of sea water. After a half hearted drying operation, which delayed us by precious minutes, we commenced our trek, stumbling occasionally across the uneven salt marshes to the low range of dunes which act, except at equinoctial tides, as a breakwater, to a strip of meres where each autumn the delicately coloured sea lavender grows in profusion, with the sandy beach immediately to the north-east.

After about twenty minutes we were crossing the dunes; soon walking out towards the edge of the receding tide. On our way we had stopped to cut and bundle marram grass for bedding our gun pits. We made our way, heavily laden with equipment, as the first signs of the new day appeared, and before our pits were constructed the edge of an orange sun peeped shyly over the eastern horizon. Our walk had warmed us but my foot was cold–surprisingly, my left foot–for the leg that was wet as a result of its immersion in salt water soon became moderately warm and remained so all through the early morning flight. As the darkness paled came the solitary note of a pinkfoot on the sand bar about one mile out to sea.

This soon increased to a soul delighting chatter. By this time we were carefully smoothing off the surrounds of the gun pits where sand had been disturbed by our excavating activities, so as to leave nothing which would attract the wily eyes of the wild geese as they came into their feeding grounds some three miles behind us.

The sun was now a blood red orb above a low layer of haze of pastel shades in deep cobalt and mauves with an upper strata of vermilion, which last colour soon extended over the lapping edge of the tide, the wet sand and the tufted sand hills behind, until the world around us was a coral tinted one. In the distance a bird was on the wing. I thought it was a pilot goose, but my momentary hope was soon dispelled, for as it approached my hide I recognised it as a black backed gull steadily floating inland at only some forty feet up. I was lazily ruminating what I could have done with it had it been a goose at that range, when the tranquility of the morning was suddenly broken by a gaggle of voices as more than two hundred pinks and greys took off from their nightly resting sanctuary on the bar.

At first sight, silhouetted against the distant bank of haze, they circled round and back only to settle again, but not for long as it proved to be a prelude, and five minutes or so later a small skein were flighting along the waters edge making due west, gaining height until with a distinct upward trend some several hundred yards from the bank of the estuary, they honked their way safely to the clover leys behind. Others came in quick succession until the morning sky seemed full, but each skein—as though on the command of its leader—pulled back their joysticks and lifted high over the usual gun emplacements. Even then, several shots rang out—ultra optimist indiscriminately shooting!

We had begun to consider the flight was over when a solitary bird—possibly a pricked one—approached at a very killable height, but it had its eyes wide open and cautiously swung away down coast. Another ten minutes and it would be 8.30. The emptiness that makes a wildfowler dream of eggs, bacon, marmalade, toast and coffee was gripping me. "Might as well pack up." I thought, but decided to wait until the half hour. One never knows. . . . wildfowling is as uncertain as it is entrancing.

Curlews began to wing their way across the now quite light and clear January sky, plaintively calling; herring gulls streamed overhead, and as I sat upright in my gun pit watching a cloud of knot twisting and twirling just above the water's edge, looking much like smoke from a passing steamer, I noticed eight geese making straight towards me. Down I dropped, my shoulder hitting my cartridge bag, which had slipped into the bottom of my shallow grave. The geese were flying dead straight as I peered very carefully over the edge. Would they keep coming on, or swing away? Ones nerves are all keyed up. . . . Surely they would not change course. . . . surely this was the opportunity come at last? Remember not to be too eager. . . . do not move until they are right over you—good advice I had so often had instilled into me.

Yes, those eight geese came—a little party of whitefronts—and I did remember those early instructions. At long last—how those seconds seemed minutes!—I was able to rise, steady myself, and as the birds swung upwards, first take the leader with my right barrel and crumple up number five with my left. The first goose did not fall stone dead, but turned back towards the sea. There was then a quarter of a mile of firm sand before the edge of the ebbing tide and he—it was a gander—could not make it.

That was my first right and left at geese. . . . a morning I shall always remember . . . not only because of this, not because of my partial nocturnal bathe, but possibly even more so on account of that wonderful coral tinted seascape as the sun crested the horizon at daybreak.

A WILDFOWLER'S LUCK

By C. Richards

Notwithstanding the appeal of the organised duck shoot or the perhaps commoner–yet even more entrancing–charms of flight shooting at moonlight night or flame coloured dawn, solitary or one companioned daylight outings sometimes produce unexpected incidents which lay claim to a place well up in the list of noteworthy occasions. A few such come readily to mind.

One is a day, some years ago now, of blustery wind and damp laden, low, scudding cloud when with a companion I set out to tramp a desolate area of wasteland. The first small bog we visited showed a fair number of snipe, but they were as wild as could be–snipe never lie well in that kind of weather–and flushed at extreme range if not mostly out of shot. Nevertheless a number were accounted for–if at a cost in cartridges that considerably lightened our bags. And then, from a mere declivity in the ground surrounded by a few sparse tufts of coarse grass, sprang three teal–but two of them not far, for our shots rang out as one and down they came very dead indeed.

It was, however, towards evening that the highlight occurred to enshrine that outing in memory. Weary, footsore and not heavily laden, we were trudging carwards when, away up in the sky flying downwind from a stretch of water hidden by a fold of the ground ahead of us, came a single duck; a shoveller, later to prove a drake in all its handsome plumage. Silhouetted there against the torn grey clouds it offered the kind of shot one dreams about; a magnificent bird to kill, and it was heading in my direction if well to the left. Perhaps my favourite shot.

Dropping to one knee, I crouched motionless, willing myself to assume the shape and appearance of some peat hags nearby. Evidently I succeeded for on came the bird until at last the psychological moment arrived; the gun butt snuggled swiftly into my shoulder and leading through and far ahead, I pressed the trigger. Up went the duck's long bill and head, back curved the graceful neck–followed by the body somersaulting over it–and life was extinct. For me the day was made, but it seemed an age before my prize thudded into the mud by the stream. It was a shot I shall not easily forget, even though it was perhaps an exceedingly lucky one.

Another occasion comes to mind; one of tempestuous south westerly gale and duck coming in from the sea, for shelter, I imagine, to a south Devonshire 'Ley.' Rocking and rolling down the wind, there seemed to be an unending stream of them, but I ran out of cartridges long before it had ended.

Still another, a day spent hidden up in a reed bed on the banks of the little River Yar in the Isle of Wight between Yarmouth and Freshwater. The tall, yellow-brown fronds rustled and whispered all about me as teal hurtled overhead. On this occasion there were two of us, each in a duck punt and some half a mile apart. All the teal in the world seemed to be congregated up that little estuary, but alas we had no dog and had to leave many of the fallen ungathered - a thing I loathe doing from every point of view.

My last goose was, strangely enough, shot when I was out pigeon decoying on a farm in the north, not far from the coast. Squatting in a ditch with decoys set up some thirty yards out in front, I had enjoyed reasonable sport when, towards late afternoon, the glorious sound of wild geese on wing sent a thrill tingling down my spine. Searching the sky to the east, I then saw them; one large and four smaller skeins of pinkfeet beating high out towards the sand bars and sea. . . . a picture to gladden any wildfowler's heart.

213

Around me on the ground the mist haze of a winter's early dust was already enshrouding the landscape (it was in fact past pigeon feed and time to go home) but up there in the sky the last rays of the sinking sun lit with warm, pinkish-gold the breasts of these great birds clamouring into the sunset. I laid aside my gun and watched in ecstasy; a sight for sore eyes. All too soon that noble company had passed, their going leaving a silence which could almost be felt. The land was hushed until, of a sudden, a faint new sound was heard–a miniature of that which had passed. It was the voice of a lone goose flying very much lower. I jerked to attention; this was something very much different; it might mean action, and I peered carefully ahead. At last I caught sight of the bird, flying straight towards me and at a height which, if it held to its course, would bring it just within range when plumb overhead.

Daring now scarcely to breath I waited; it might be, I conjectured, a pricked bird–the victim of some flight shooter's foray–separated from the main flocks and unable to catch up. Nearer and nearer it came, straight as a die; not only was its sonorous *ung-unk–ung-unk*! clearly audible but the sound of its wing beats too. Fifteen seconds, ten, five, two–*now*! and I fired just before my barrels reached the vertical. Some shooting men assert that the striking of pellets on a bird in the air cannot be heard. I disagree, and I certainly heard those, but possibly not the few which were fatal and killed it. The goose faltered momentarily; then with wing beats rapidly accelerating it began climbing–and turning back on its original track. I knew it was hard hit but already out of range of a second barrel. Up and up it went, higher and higher until having completed a full 180 degrees turn, abruptly the great pinions stopped thrashing, the powerful neck appeared to collapse and crumple back over its body. With wings now semi-folded it keeled over, slithering earthwards.

I did not see it actually hit the ground; that was impossible for it fell a quarter of a mile back; but there it lay, a huge grey form out on the plough land waiting to be gathered. Maybe it was, and will be, my last goose, but I shall not forget it nor the occasion

Finally, a picture from Ireland: a waste of green-brown bogland and blue, distant mountains and a long V-shaped wedge of greylag geese patterning the winter sky. Crouched down below them in a 'pill' or runnel of a tidal river, I watched them suddenly break formation and tumble 'anyhow' out of the sky. 'Whiffling' this is called, and down they came until, when only a few feet up they saw me, and with an incredible roar of wings climbed steeply away.

No thought, I am glad to say, occurred to me of shooting!

CRIPPLE STOPPING

By Captain Lacy (1842)

In gunners' language, those birds which are wounded but which do not fly away after having been shot at, are called 'cripples,' and as most wild birds, when not very severely struck, are extremely alert and cunning. If the gunner calculates positively on having to find canoe-room for all his cripples, he will but too frequently discover that he "has been reckoning without his host." Hence the necessity for the 'cripple-chase' by land and water, and of those useful auxiliaries in this noble science–the 'cripple stopper' and the 'cripple net.'

The cripple net is in principle, the angler's landing net applied to the raising of fowl, instead of fish, from the surface of the water; for which purpose it was first used by Colonel Hawker, who appears to marvel, as well he may, that no one "till November, 1832," had ever thought of the plan. The Colonel gives a very just description of the great advantages of this net to the gunner, and also a description of the dimensions of the one he recommends, and which, no doubt, answers the purpose very well.

I prefer, however, a copper hoop much less in diameter, and a net smaller in the mesh than his; because the hoop is stiffer, sinks quicker–is altogether more handy to use and stow away, and is yet quite sufficiently wide at the top to take the largest fowl. With smaller meshes the net hangs better, especially when made, as it ought to be, with a long tail, in order to catch up three or four ducks one after the other, in quick succession, as you scud past them, under sail. Before you take in the net enclosing the birds, you should always give it a shake or two overboard, to dislodge the wet.

If a cripple pop up from under or alongside the canoe, and dive *instanter*, as frequently is the case, you may often take him when you do not even see him, by observing the direction of his head when he goes under water, and then by darting the net in, overhand, a short distance before him. There is some skill to be shown in aiming with the net as well below as above the surface.

The best cripple stopper I should say, is the heaviest double–for a double it always ought to be–that the shooter can wield with perfect ease and quickness; and the same gun will answer for flight shooting also. It should be got up in a plain way, with brass or German-silver mounting; should always be thinly coated with neat's foot oil; should be frequently washed out, and when not in use, kept at all times near to a fire and free from damp. Some gunners have the stock and even the barrel painted white, which certainly is the least conspicuous colour when you are afloat.

In places where the water is shallow, and the tides weak, you may manage to kill cripples with almost any sort of gun; but where there are channels and hot tides, you ought to have one, which when required will reach them at long distances, and when even the use of Eley's cartridges will often be found anything but false economy. In my opinion, cripple shooting in its various forms is excellent practice for a young gunner, besides being, at times, very good sport.

A small charge of loose shot in the right barrel, and one of Eley's cartridges in the left, is the best general mode of loading, but, of course, you must vary the charge according to circumstances. When waddings are used, always use punched ones, for expedition's sake. If compelled to use but one kind, Eley's blue cartridges, which require no wadding, would be the best, and whenever there is much swell or 'lipper on,' always load with the stock placed perpendicularly in the centre of the canoe, so that if your gun or powder flask slip from your hand, neither go overboard, nor do you lose your equilibrium. I once lost a new powder flask, nearly full of powder, from neglecting to attend to this precaution. Short barrels suit a cripple stopper the best, even though it be a heavy gun. Two feet seven or eight inches is the best size, as you can load whilst kneeling on one knee, the steadiest position when there is much motion. Besides, they are less affected by the wind, and are in every way, more handy in a canoe.

When afloat, never place a loaded gun in such position that if it were to go off the charge would pass through any part of the canoe. The muzzle of your small gun should rest on a copper hook, or in a copper ring fixed on the combings on the starboard side, so that it is thus elevated above the front deck. The but-end should rest against a chock of wood, nailed with copper nails on to the bottom boards to prevent the gun from slipping down, and which should be so secured that it cannot be shaken out of its place. The barrels and locks are protected from wet by means of a short canvas curtain, nailed on to the combings with copper tacks, and then painted white. An oiled Russia-duck gun cover is a great additional protection.

Having now given a description of the two implements so essential in a cripple chase, I beg to conduct my readers to an actual participation in the sport itself.

The principal points in manoeuvring cripples are:- 1st. To go about the matter in the likeliest way to secure the most, and if possible, the whole of them in the shortest space of time.

2nd. To use the net whenever you judiciously can in order to prevent the noise of a report, to preserve the birds themselves from being further injured with shot, and to save ammunition.

3rd. To lose not a moment in hoisting sail whenever it can be used with advantage and especially when the wind is such as to admit of the man managing the sail and sculling at the same time, because you are then perfectly at liberty to use the oar, the gun, or the net, as each may be required, and frequently each is required, and in very quick succession too.

Cripple Chase on the Water.

After having made a shot with the large gun, go up first to the dead birds, which generally will, and nearly always ought to, exceed your cripples. As you approach within shoulder gun shot, be ready with the gun as some of those apparently dead or *in extremis* may be more lively in reality than they appear to be. If you observe any swimming 'bold' and looking suspiciously at you, as soon as you are well within shot, let drive first with one barrel and then with the other, 'standing to no repairs.' Then, out with the cripple net and make sure of the dead ones, because one bird in the canoe is worth two on the water, and dead birds are soon boated.

This done, if you deem it expedient to follow them at all, instantly give chase to those which are making out the farthest from the shore, and then to those which have gone along shore against the wind, because the sail will soon carry you down upon the remainder afterwards. But if the bulk of the cripples be making in for shore, it will generally be the best policy to pursue them, as without a dog or a following boat you will in all probability lose some of them on the mud, whilst they will stand no chance of escape in the shallow water.

When a bird swims 'corky' and bold, he is hit in the body, neck or head, and may be either recovering fast and ready for a start, or may be inwardly bleeding to death and thus it is sometimes remarkable that birds which you had observed but a moment before sitting upright and to all appearances perfectly well, suddenly droop their heads, flap their wings on the water and expire. But if wing broke they swim deep and these for the most part are the cripples that dive so plaguily, and which shew you–especially if pinioned only–the most antics and give you the most trouble. They sometimes swim for perhaps 200 or 300 yards with no more than the end of their bills out of the water, which is just dribbling over their backs. All you can see of them looks no bigger than a mouse, not very easy to distinguish on a ruffled surface.

If a bird, when you first approach him, dives and comes up fresh and lively and especially if he keep long under water before he again shows himself, and gain upon you in the chase, shoot him as soon as you can, particularly if you have other cripples about. It is a pity to put extra pellets into a bird where it can be avoided but it is better to do so than not to get him at all, and to lose others into the bargain. I have lost numbers of birds by trying the cripple net too long, having a mortal aversion to using the gun a second time where it can be avoided. This is one of the great excellencies of the cripple net. With it you can catch up a pinioned bird or one but slightly wounded, which without the net you would have been compelled to have shot. In the former instance the bird would be valuable as a present, in the latter it might have received half the contents of one of Eley's 'Blues.'

The gunner that shows his cripples the least quarter will in the long run get more of them than will the merciful and sparing one. But at the same time he should never blow a bird to atoms, but wait for his second appearance at a distance, or let the canoe drift from him and then fire. That is to say, if you can afford the time, if not, aim aside and do him as little damage as you can. Recollect too, that a bird which is much shot bleeds profusely and spoils the appearance of others in the canoe.

When you have a wary, dodging, quick diving cripple to deal with who just pops up and then down again, let your man look one way and you another, for four eyes are none too many here, so that if possible he may not jockey you. Thus you have a double chance of keeping him in view and ultimately of bagging him. The best way, when you expect him to show himself is to bring your gun up- for it is the motion of your arms in doing this which most alarms the bird–to the shoulder, with the finger on the trigger and fire the instant he appears. This is very smart popping on both sides and if the reader fancy it tame work and so mighty easy, let him try it and then let him declare whether snap shots in the field or on the water are the more difficult, even with the advantage of the gun to the shoulder and especially if the motion of the boat be not very steady. Before now I have seen a little teal after as many as half a dozen successive well meant shots at his diminutive exterior, pop up his tiny figure, looking as sly and lively as a stoat in a rabbit warren.

Cripple Chase on Land or Sand.

After making a successful shot, as it is generally advisable for one hand to stay in the canoe to take care of her, to keep her afloat and thus prevent the water splashing over her and as it would frequently be dangerous for both hands to go ashore, the best mode of managing is this:- Leaving the man in charge of the canoe, take the double and shoot those cripples first that take wing and then those which are either making for, or have already toddled into the water. Leave the dead ones, and slipping the necks of such as are not dead, or are evidently past all hope of recovery, drop them down instantly as you despatch them.

Those birds which sit or stand moping with the feathers all ruffled on their heads are generally hit in the head or eye only and are not to be trusted as they sometimes recover and take sudden leave of you. It is the best plan, therefore, to despatch them also. Now make the best of your way to the others which are making the best of *their* way, I can assure you, across the sand or mud to creeks and other water, pursuing those the first which will be the first to reach the channels as you can afterwards make sure play at those in the shallows and small creeks. When, however, there is no danger of the canoe filling, drifting away, or grounding unfavourably, then draw her ashore and help each other to collect the birds, one with the cripple net in hand attending to those at home and the other with the gun pursuing the stragglers. This mode always prevents loss of time and frequently, loss of birds.

When your cripples are thus pacing it over the sand at a distance and you observe one or more of them attempt to fly, but which clearly—from having been pinioned or wing tipped—cannot rise above a few inches from the ground, lay down your gun if the sand be dry and perhaps doff your jacket and run after them. This will keep you fresh for the heats. If the tide be coming in rapidly you must of course, be cautious where you lay your gun down, particularly if the man do not see you in the act.

All the annas tribe, or at all events gray geese, widgeon, duck and teal, especially the latter, when crippled at low water are wont to keep skulking out at the channel sides and after running from thirty to 100 yards or more, lay themselves down with outstretched necks so close to the ground between the ridges of the sand, that it is sometimes no easy matter to see them and at all times they are liable thus to be mistaken for a lump of wreck, &c.

The collection of ten or a dozen teal in this way, will give any man in a gunning dress a thorough good warming. But it may be said that common sense and the birds themselves will teach a man all this and so they may in time. But I am vain enough to imagine that the unpracticed gunner who does me the honour to repose confidence in my practical instructions so far as to deem them worthy a place under his gunning cap, will derive early advantages from them, more than sufficient to compensate the trouble of having imbibed them.

GLORIOUS MUD

By. J. Pearce

"Mud, mud, glorious mud,
Nothing quite like it for cooling the blood."

So goes the old ditty. In my particular case it is not so glorious and quite definitely it had the reverse effect on my blood, and this is what happened.

The local reports were good, the ducks were about in numbers; my wildfowling friend and I immediately got into a huddle to get at them. The plan was worked on a hunch. The arrangements were for us to be at a spot at least thirty minutes before flighting time, and settle down in our usual place behind a bank which overlooked a gulley, where it was anticipated the ducks would be. At first light we would then up and over on to the mud, spreading out at a good angle in order to get a good first shot.

We also knew if the birds were there they would, after the

227

first shots, fly into the long gulley, climb and return over us; therefore we arranged to stay put after the initial cartridges had been fired, thenceforth to give them a parting shot. This plan was formulated on the eve prior to the proposed outing. Weather reports were good, spring flood tide in our favour for retrieving as we had no dog; in fact everything was just right. Crossing our fingers we hoped that the ducks would not disappoint us.

Early the next morning, fortified with steaming porridge and tea we set out full of optimism. After walking a well known mile of scrub, creeks and everything which makes wildfowling easy!, we arrived quietly at our pre-arranged destination and settled down in plenty of time to the tune of whistling teal and widgeon, and the occasional call of mallard and shoveller. The curlew present were gurgling, a good sign that they were settled and had not been disturbed by our approach. This, so far, was it, and we could hardly suppress our excitement. We eagerly awaited sufficient light to see what the score was as far as numbers and distribution were concerned.

Gradually a beautiful dawn broke, and, raising my head cautiously above the bank I could distinguish the shapes of ducks dibbling, preening and generally fussing around the water's edge. I'm sure they could hear my pulse! I whispered to my friend to get set. Slowly rising on one knee we loaded our guns and made sure the safety catches were on; then at the given signal we hopped over the bank in our respective directions on to the mud. With a tremendous whirr of wings and calls of alarm they clawed for sky. A right brought down a widgeon. A miss to the left–to this day, I don't know why! I reloaded quickly as, as anticipated they flew up the gulley and turned to flight out. Two more birds fell to my friend's gun. All was going very well, but I was soon to be sadly disillusioned.

During the time I had reached my position on the mud and fired my first shots I was well down and not unduly worried, but during the ensuing few minutes of exciting flighting I had sunk further, too far to be comfortable. My friend doing his retrieving was by this time up on hard ground about twenty five yards away. I shouted that I was stuck. "You'll be alright," he called and promptly disappeared. I assumed to pick up another bird. By this time I was truly in up to my thighs. It was impossible to move my legs or slip my thigh boots. I could only twist at my trunk and this made matters worse, so I decided to remain perfectly still. By this time I was perspiring freely despite the cold weather.

Again I shouted to my partner that I could not move. Along he came and replied that he would lend a hand, unloaded, laid down his gun and out he came, but he too began to sink. He immediately dropped on his hands and knees and crawled to me, and offered his shoulder for leverage, but to no avail. He was sinking adjacent to the mess I had made. He tried again but the mud was now churned up around us to a black, oozy, vile smelling glue. I told him to go back out of it before it was too late, and seek assistance from the neighbouring farm nearly a mile away. He took one look at the tide line which was by this time about six yards from us and, before departing, assured me all would be well.

About five minutes later my only hope returned dragging tree branches. These he dragged to me and placed them round me as best he could. With his assistance and all the strength I could muster in my arms, the struggle began. Encouraged by my friend I exerted a final effort and gradually, very gradually I came out. The branches had proved their worth.

Utterly exhausted and bathed in perspiration I flopped forward to recover. I must have looked a pitiful sight covered with black slime, crawling up the mud to the safety of terra-firma. My friend came up in the rear (with my gun) to ensure I made the grade. I had no further enthusiasm to shoot any more. I was very thankful indeed and extremely grateful for the assistance I had been given. Our total bag, three widgeon, one teal and, definitely not as planned—a mud bath! Fellow 'fowlers will call us fools for not using mud patterns. I for one have not used them on recommendation from my very experienced partner who swears that they are a menace, especially in our locality where the gullies are steep and they become dangerous skis.

THE MUD TRAP

By R. Arnold

The coastal gunner has to watch many things besides the habits of and behaviour of the birds he shoots. He has to take notice of tide times and heights, to watch the changing contours of the marsh, the moving patches of soft sand, the onset of fog. Neglect to take any precautions relating to these matters can be fatal, or if not fatal, extremely terrifying. Perhaps it may also mean that other people may have to risk their lives needlessly to save the careless sportsman.

It needs little imagination to picture the terrible, slow death, which sometimes overtakes the fowler trapped by tide, or fog, or quicksand—perhaps a combination of all three. Perhaps, mercifully, a madness comes before the end, but the terrible, helpless loneliness of it all is awful to contemplate.

One of my habits has always been to treat the marshes and mudflats with respect. I did neglect to obey an old fowler's prediction concerning fog in my younger days, and the horrible scare I had in consequence made me much wiser. I used to enjoy excellent wigeon flighting and wader shooting over a certain estuary before the war. This estuary was blessed with hard, clean sands which made fowling much easier than some of the muddy spots I have sported over before and since the occurrence I am about to relate.

At the mouth of a big gutter, about a mile from the saltings, the hard sands rose slowly to a little island of mussel scar. Though submerged by several feet at high water, it drained off remarkably well and made a comfortable spot from which to shoot. When the mussel scar was surrounded it was possible to wade back to the big gutter quite comfortably, at the most knee deep, even when the wind raised the tide a little. There was never any danger there as the gunner could get ashore to high ground even when washed off the mussel scar! The sand was completely unbroken by any gutters or dikes and so the splash back was made in complete comfort.

However, like many another gunner, I had to forsake the wild saltings and mudflats during the war years, to seek a more formidable quarry. During those periods in the Services and overseas I often yearned for the chance to shoot my marsh again and when demobbing came I took the first available chance, although my home was now well away from the district, and went back.

It seemed the same. Here and there barbed wire fences fringed gutters and ringed the sea wall. Nissen huts had sprung up in the hinterland, and concrete pill boxes were somewhat obviously placed along the wall itself. The saltings seemed the same, the main channel or gutter had straightened itself a little, some of the more familiar bends and shallow bays, where curlew and teal congregated had disappeared. It was a little deeper too, as the old, familiar fords had gone. That I soon found when I commenced to wade it.

The mussel scar was still there, albeit smaller, and the trip across the hard sands seemed the same. Probably a little softer, but I put that down to an increase in *anno domini* and the fact that I was out of fowling training. I made my slit trench, as usual, in the mussel scar and waited for the flight, without success, and decided to hang on and wait for the rising tide to push the waders off the distant flats, and indulge in a little tidal shooting. Things went according to plan. The tide rose, at the same old rate, the curlews and shanks and plover came in the old familiar way, and I took my sport with the usual amount of success, and the equally usual amount of misses.

I looked behind me. The tide was flowing softly over the

sands–there was no wind and it was smooth as a mirror's surface. I decided it was time to go back. It was nearly a mile back to the saltings and after I had covered the first 100 yards, with water round my ankles, I realised the pickle I was in. Where before the sands had been hard under the tide, now they were soft and clinging; soft underwater mud in its worst form! It should take me, normally, about 15 to 20 minutes to get back to the big gutter. By that time the water was generally up to 18 inches deep. Today it was different.

After I had floundered some further 100 yards or so, I realised that I was going to be lucky indeed to make the distant shore with nothing worse than a wet bottom. The water was only an inch or so deep, but I was already sinking halfway up to the knee in the mud with each step. I could not stop to puzzle it out, I had to keep going. I glanced behind me–the mussel scar was still well above water. I pushed on, or rather floundered on again. Fifty yards and then the going became a little easier. The sand was harder and the total immersion was about to my calf. Then disaster!

A few more steps and I was over my knees in soft mud, each step a sucking, dragging horror. And the water was rising slowly and steadily. The shore looked even further away than ever. This was no time for panicking, so I trudged on, sinking deeper and deeper until when I had panted and wheezed and splashed a further couple of hundred yards the water was over the tops of my waders. Well over a half mile to go and mud bound, immersed over the waders, thoroughly exhausted, and not a little frightened, I again struck a hard patch and splashed on, almost in a run, with the water round my knees. Again a soft patch and a nightmare it was, fully a quarter of a mile of it with the water at my chest and every step a long agony of sinking and perspiring extrication.

I didn't feel the cold of the water, only the weight and pressure of it. I forgot, in my personal anxiety, to rid myself of the wet and sodden cartridges cluttering up my pockets. I remembered to hold my gun aloft, and hung my waders around my neck. Again, fortunately, the going became easier, but though the sand was harder, my progress had been so slow that with 200 yards to go I was waist deep. The muds again became soft and sticky, but I was past caring.

Plunging into it, struggling out only to plunge as deep with the next step, I finally made the edge of the salting, against the high mud wall of it fringed with marsh plants, with the water almost at my neck. Heaving myself up the steep muddy, slippery sides, with my waders full of water, my clothing sodden and heavy with the tide, and physically exhausted, was a terrific exertion. I managed it with my heart thudding in my chest and blood pounding in a roar round my ears, then lay, soaked as I was, on the damp green grasses, to try to recover some strength.

At last I recovered sufficiently to make my way off the saltings to a marsh side farm where the good wife took away my wet clothes and dried them in the oven. A good cup of hot sweet tea, and bacon and eggs (farmhouse style) revived me, and after the tide had ebbed I went out again on to the saltings to look at the scene of my frantic escape.

Then I saw the reason for it all. Throughout the seven years I had been away, the rains and tides and wind and forces of erosion had been at work. The mussel scar had been built up with sand and mud, the long, flat sands had become saucer shaped. That was one reason why the water rushed in more quickly, one reason why the muds did not drain off so quickly as before and so were more soft and ooze-like. I had been lucky. Had it been night or in fog I might not have fared so well. I had a good scare, I lost a box of cartridges I could ill afford to loose, but I had learned a valuable lesson.

Never underestimate the marshes–always, *always* without exception study them carefully and do not take one year's observations as to contours and dangerous patches as sufficient information to carry on blithely in the following year. One other thing. In my pack, when I go fowling, I now carry an R.A.F. inflatable rubber dinghy. It only weighs a few ounces—certainly less than 25 cartridges—it makes an excellent flighting pit for sinking in soft mud, it makes an excellent seat (when folded) for flighting from and, above all, it is my personal answer to the challenge of deep gutters and treacherous channels.

I only hope that the lesson I learned the hard way that day may be of guidance perhaps to some tyro about to tackle the great, lonely, treacherous muds alone.

DUCK SHOOTING FROM THE AVON "GAZES"

By R. Hargreaves (1903)

There is no more attractive and exciting way of shooting wildfowl than that which has been developed on the Hampshire Avon and Stour. They are slow-flowing, weedy rivers flanked by wide water meadows with broad ditches, and the quietness and amount of food attracts ducks of many kinds in large numbers.

By ordinary methods it would be difficult to get more than a very moderate bag, but to overcome this difficulty a system has been devised of shooting out of what are termed "gazes." A portion of the river bank, say from 200 to 600 yards in length, which is known to be a favourite haunt of the duck, is screened by putting up a high post and rail fence a few feet from the bank, and filling it in with green boughs such as fir, gorse, or rhododendron, till quite impervious. In this the gazes, which are very similar to grouse driving boxes, are made, so that you can get into them without being seen by any fowl that are on the water. Unless the gazes are a considerable distance apart, they should be on the same side of the river, as otherwise the shooting would be hampered.

If there are willows growing beside the gazes, they must be carefully trimmed, so that a clear space is left in front, but a good deal of covert left at the sides, or the ducks will see you as they fly up and down the stream. The fence helps to attract the fowl, as it not only shelters them from the wind, but prevents their being "stared at," which they particularly dislike; and if there are willows; so much the better, as the branches stretching out into the stream break the current and make comfortable resting places for them. The usual plan is to have three sets of gazes, and each set is occupied twice during the day.

Of course the length of the portions screened off and the distances apart vary considerably. Sometimes they are so near together that it is surprising the ducks are not put away from one set of gazes by the firing at the next, but if they are well out of sight they are not easily moved. Perhaps the best way of explaining the method is to describe a day's shooting:

The guns, generally four or five, go down to within a few hundred yards of the first gazes. The host or keeper takes out his watch and says, "Are you ready to take the time?" Then, "Seven minutes from now." That is, that you are all to be in your allotted gazes in seven minutes, which is the time it will take the gun who has the one farthest off to reach it, and no shot must be fired before the time is up. You walk off with your loader. Sometimes there are posts put in the meadows 100 yards from each gaze, and you wait there till one minute before time. Then you creep, watch in hand, towards your gaze; ten seconds more and you are only five yards outside. You wait a moment, then walk into the gaze, still crouching; and if you are wise wait for someone else to fire the first shot, so that you at least cannot be blamed for spoiling the show.

The moment the first shot goes you stand erect. Out fly some half a dozen mallard. You miss the first from shooting under him as he rises, kill the second, and then plaster two more that have only just risen, as they had to swim several yards to get clear of the willows; then miss one and wound one rather far over towards the other side of the river. That is all for the moment, and you crouch down to wait for some flying round.

How many shots are missed from not straightening oneself after one has been crouching to keep out of sight! Try an imaginary shot crouching even slightly, and see how helpless you are. Here come two mallard! How high are they? A hundred and fifty feet! They look tempting, but do not shoot. You are not very likely to kill one, and you will put all the ducks on the wing within a quarter of a mile up one storey higher, and spoil sport for the other guns. It requires a good deal of judgement and unselfishness to hold one's hand from these sky high birds, but if you want to make a bag it must be done.

A few more shots and the drive is over, as the fowl are almost all mallard and soon leave. Easy shooting you think it at present, and so it is, but, as Mesty said, "Stop a little!" The picking-up men are coming up the river, two in a punt and one on each bank, with a retriever and gun, to stop the divers. You leave your gaze and meet the other guns again half a mile further up. Out come the watches. "Eleven minutes please, gentlemen."

This time you get into your gaze a minute before time. Carefully you peep through a chink in the fir boughs, and your heart beats faster as you see over a hundred wigeon and teal scattered over the river, here some fifty yards wide. How disgusted you would be if they all rose before the time was up! You pick out the thickest clump of wigeon, and the instant the first shot sounds, shoot at them sitting with your first barrel and flying with the second, and then for half an hour you have as fine a bit of shooting as any one can wish for–all heights, all angles, and all paces, for the wind is blowing hard upstream.

The willows hamper you a little, and you wish for eyes in the back of your head, for several times you hear a whistle of wings, and a single teal going 150 miles an hour down wind is past you and almost out of shot before you can snap one barrel at it. I know nothing more difficult than to kill one's second barrel out of a bunch of teal well on the wing. The first shot is more or less straight forward, but the moment that it is fired the bunch bursts like a shell in all directions, some rising almost straight into the air at marvellous speed, and you must be very clever indeed if you can guess in what direction your second barrel is likely to be fired.

The wigeon, as a rule, fly higher and rather more steadily, and are easier to deal with. One grasps some of the difficulty of the shooting by watching birds going to the other guns, and seeing how quickly they twist aside or upwards the instant they are shot at, and often even the moment the shooter begins to put his gun up. Here comes a single wigeon some 70 feet up; just as you are going to pull, it does a switchback, shooting down close to the surface of the river just in front of you, and up again at lightning speed. You miss both barrels, and are perhaps consoled by knowing that you did not shoot anywhere near the bird, and that you could only have hit it by a fluke. It is very hard to say whether you should shoot at wounded ducks; it is true, they may give a good deal of trouble in picking up, but on the other hand, you may take ducks from the other guns by firing. It is best, at all events, not to fire unnecessary shots early in the rise.

Again you move up the river, and this time you have to walk three quarters of a mile, and the time given is sixteen minutes. You turn on to some wild healthy ground, with occasional patches of grass nibbled short by the rabbits, which look as if they ought to be golf greens, and then down again into the water meadows. When you get into your gaze you find it is placed in a long narrow osier bed opposite a wider reach of the river, so that any bird flying up the opposite bank is a long way out. Here you get half a dozen shots at snipe. Some skimming over the river like swallows make very instructive shooting, as you can tell, by the strike of the pellets on the water, exactly where you put the middle of the charge. Some come over very high, and these, I think, are often missed by shooting too far in front of them. A snipe rises very quickly and is going at his best pace before you can get your gun on to him, but I do not believe he ever flies any faster than he does when he is 20 yards from where he rose, and I have often noticed how long a rocketing snipe seems to be in coming to you, and how slowly he goes out of sight.

This time some of the keepers have gone a mile up the river to drive down the coots that have been collecting there, and you presently see some black specks come sailing steadily down the valley at all heights–50 feet, 100 feet, 150 feet. You can either begin at the lowest and work up to the highest, or begin at the highest in the hope of hitting off the range at once; but if you want to feel pleased with your shooting at the end of the drive, I advise the former course. Then come lunch, and then the three beats over again, with, of course, fewer fowl.

Such a day has many attractions. The chance of getting rare ducks, such as shoveller, pintail, golden-eye, etc; the uncertainty of the sport, for so much depends on the weather and the difficulty of the shooting. Contrary to general experience, the shooting at teal and wigeon–and they are the birds that provide the best sport–is often more difficult on a still day than on a windy one, as the latter seems to steady them, and stop their turning and rising and dropping so quickly, and that is what really beats a good shot even when in form.

To turn to individual days and bags, 800 ducks have been killed in four days' shooting, there being, of course, considerable intervals between the days to allow the ducks to settle in. Some years since, the late Mr. John Mills of Bisterne, with an 8-bore and a 12, in flood time killed 130 fowl to his own gun in a day, remaining the whole day in the same gaze.

The most remarkable piece of shooting of this class, however, with which the writer is acquainted, was done three years ago at Avon Tyrrell, Lord Manners' place, close to the ford across which, according to tradition, Sir Walter Tyrell fled after the murder of King Rufus. One of the guns went into the lowest gaze with 100 cartridges. In a very short time he had fired them all away, knocking down over 60 ducks, and then had to stand in his gaze with two empty guns for half an hour, with swarms of ducks flying all round him. he told the writer he was sure he could have doubled his score if he had had enough cartridges. Ten days afterwards the writer went into the same gaze full of hope and loaded with cartridges. He came out of it after having fired just six shots!

It is always rather an exciting moment when approaching this particular gaze, as you have to cross some rather higher ground to get at it, and there are often flocks of fowl in full view of you in a kind of lagoon at the ford. One hears them whistling and calling, and now and then a bunch will get up and fly round two or three times before settling again, and one nervously wonders if all the rest will join them and go away;

but perhaps they are used to seeing people moving about, as the river here is close to a high road and some cottages, and they seldom seem to leave till they are shot at.

I am not one of those who have much faith in large shot for this kind of shooting, or indeed any kind except rabbits at short ranges. Of course, occasionally a big pellet may break a pinion or give a blow that will bring down a bird that would have gone on if hit by a smaller pellet; but in these cases the bird would probably dive and give much trouble to recover, and particularly in the case of high shots overhead, when the neck and head are the only really vulnerable parts, and offers such a very small mark, the increased number of pellets in a charge of say No. 6 gives you a much better chance of hitting it. I remember a case in point, when a friend of mine, a first rate shot, went over for a day's shooting in Perthshire. On arriving he found that, instead of shooting grouse, they were to drive capercailzie. The men in the house had been loading cartridges overnight with all kinds of weird charges—50 grains of powder, shot as big as peas, etc. However, to their surprise his ordinary cartridges with No. 6 shot seemed to kill the capercailzie much cleaner and further off than all their fancy loads.

The mode of shooting I have been describing might, I think,

be adopted in many other places with satisfactory results. As long as you can keep the water quiet–and the fencing in of the banks, which is not really an expensive business, to a great extent ensures this quiet–the ducks will come in and stay in. In the case of the Avon and Stour there is a great amount of food, and this largely helps to attract and keep the fowl; but there are many other rivers and streams where the feeding is good, and it may be supplemented by artificial feeding, such as throwing acorns, of which the duck are particularly fond, into the water.

In many cases I believe it would answer to keep a small piece of the river, say half a mile, as a sanctuary where no shot was to be fired. I have shot at a place in Suffolk where such a sanctuary was made, and the way the ducks used to flock into it, although there was a man walking up and down all the time to put them out, used to make one's mouth water. You cannot have many days–four or five a year at the outside–or you never get a really good bag, and of course, you are very dependent on the weather, but when successful there is no better, and certainly no cheaper, sport.

SOME GOOSE TALK

By J. Jones

I am never quite sure what exactly is the real fascination of goose shooting, or more often a wild goose chase, but for me at any rate and I hope for many others, it is little short of magic.

Goose routine is far more varied than one would think. I live in a part of Scotland where "home" to the geese, or at least sleeping quarters, is the mouth of an estuary. There is a morning chorus of arrangements, fresh arrangements and indecisions until the moment for "jumping" comes and the journey is made to the finally chosen feeding ground by the majority of the flock. Another home during the autumn, the open part of the winter and the spring is one of several lochs, while a third is much higher up a tidal estuary, each with the same feeding routine. When a freeze-up occurs, the inland birds have no choice but to take to salt water or salt marshes beyond the reach of man and gun. There is no punt gunning here.

To me a goose is one of the most lordly and majestic of birds, whose music and form are delights to the ear and eye. Gaining contact with him is a perpetual and fascinating puzzle. To get within shooting range requires a low tide to let one nose far out into a tidal creek, and a headwind sufficiently strong to keep them down to a reasonable height. But woe betide the shooter who waits too long. I have had to swim for it with an unexpectedly high tide and it is not an experience to be repeated.

In the evening, flighting on to the inland lochs, they spiral down from a thousand feet or more with a glorious display of aerobatics and in the mornings, on their way to the finally chosen feeding ground, rise rapidly before crossing the shore against the chance of a concealed shooter, to a height where nothing short of an anti-aircraft gun would avail. There only remains their feeding grounds on which to get to grips with them and who shall forecast where those will be on a particular day?

There are, of course, some good pointers–first the stubble and then the "tattie" fields after their crops have been lifted, particularly after a touch of frost and rain which helps to soften and rot the rejects which have been left lying on the ground. These fields, of course, are often in an area where game is preserved and the holders of the sporting rights have little reason to risk interference with their birds, and it is naturally not an easy task immediately to establish one's bona-fides with strangers who well know the temptation of a covey of partridges or a pheasant after hours of fruitless waiting for a goose which has taken another turning.

I have always found the owner-farmer to be the most cooperative and an assurance (rigorously kept) of "geese only" will usually bring the desired permission–particularly as a large number of geese will do a great deal of damage in a very short time to young crops in the spring of the year. The farmer, too, can very often be of the greatest help because he knows what is likely to be the feeding area, or at least where they have fed in previous years, as it is indeed a fact that for some reason geese will insist on feeding in one particular area year after year within a given acreage of say 1000 to 3000 acres, but will seldom of their own choice go to apparently wholly desirable places outside these same areas.

At the same time, it always seems to me that it is such a chancy business choosing exactly the right spot, that one should go to a little extra trouble to take every possible care–a hide takes only a very short time to make but pays a huge dividend if the field on which it looks is the favoured spot. Depending on the colour of the background, it is often worth while to darken face and hands. If you have ever looked down from an aeroplane on an upturned human face, you will understand. You just cannot help but see it–or any sudden movement. It is an inborn instinct, a matter of life and death, from the goose's point of view.

The last time I went out, I found an old tattie field on the upper slopes of a low range of hills where I had seen a number of pinkfeet feeding over a period of a day or two. They kept just out of shot of the boundary fences but did not seem to mind feeding near the "hods" of potatoes in one corner of the field, so, as the moon was almost full, I enlisted the aid of Tom and Alistair and we disposed ourselves, Alistair behind the hods, Tom in a hide I had made in the fence between the old tattie field and a very likely stubble, and myself with a roving commission. We got into position about seven o'clock, just as the moon rose, and almost at the same moment the first goose was heard. But as usual they had changed their minds once again and came over, skein after skein from ten to thirty strong, just out of shot and away into the distance. Alistair killed a widgeon after it was apparent that no geese were going to land and we had no choice but to abandon the project, and made the best of a thermos flask of hot coffee laced with that most estimable and renowned product of Scotland.

Tom, however, was determined not to be foiled, so on the next day, being Sunday, he and I drew a line on the map in the direction in which they had been flighting and motored along it as far as the country lanes and farm roads would permit. After about eight miles motoring and walking we suddenly found them feeding in a huge tattie field which, after careful reconnaissance, we decided was a workable proposition. I spent the remainder of the evening getting in touch with the farmer who owned it, and finally got his blessing for an all-out effort the following night. During Sunday night snow fell, not enough to cover the ground, but filling up the remains of the old furrows and leaving only the tops of what had been ridges their natural colour. It froze as well and the snow that had fallen would obviously lie.

On Monday night we met near the farm and after parking our cars, walked to the field. It was freezing hard and an icy wind was blowing. I had put on a pair of long white pants and an old whitish pyjama jacket over my clothes by way of camouflage and found some white material with which to cover the top of my cap. Tom had done the same but Alistair had kept to darker clothing. We decided, therefore that he should keep in the cover of a boundary wall on the flight line, while Tom and I lay out in the field. While we were still deciding the best positions to take up in the field, we were greatly pleased to find the foot marks in the snow of a great many geese, then the first "Ka-wa-wak" sounded and we took up our battle positions.

The moon had not yet risen and I am sure we were quite invisible from the air so long as we remained still. Under such circumstances, where there is a possibility of a large number of geese coming in to feed, I have found that it is always advisable to let the first party come right in. If they settle even within shot, so much the better. If the pathfinders are shot at and live to return to the main flock and tell the tale, I am certain that it can seriously influence the rest of the flight. On this occasion there was little need for holding back as they came in quick succession. Tom fired first, missed with his right and was rewarded with a resounding "thump" on the ground after his left. I, meanwhile, found that I was rather on the outside of their turning circle, so moved in a bit, handsomely missed a single bird and then killed one.

I had foolishly carried my bag containing a flask of soup, cartridges, torch, and other things into the open with me and in a half lying position had found it too cumbersome to wear so had taken it off. As I went to pick up my bird some forty yards away, the main body started to arrive. Tom had several more shots and was suitably rewarded. I also fired again without success and put my hand into my coat pocket for more cartridges. Horror of horrors, they were all in my bag except two! I tried vainly to work out just where I had left it, but it had vanished completely. I then fired my remaining two cartridges at six birds which came over me nicely–only one dropped out and planed down about a hundred yards away– and I had no more cartridges. It seemed essential to pick this bird up at once as it looked suspiciously like a runner, so I chased away after it.

During the next ten minutes at least three hundred to five hundred birds floated round and round my head at zero feet and there was nothing to be done about it. At last I found the bird (stone dead) and also Alistair from whom I got a handful of cartridges. Having little opportunity to shoot where he was, he also advanced into the field and almost at once killed a bird. At that moment the moon rose from behind a belt of fir trees that bounded the eastern side of the field. It was, I think, the most wonderful sight I have ever seen with well over five hundred geese in full chorus circling round the area and silhouetted against the sky and rising moon.

When one sees geese flighting I am always reminded of Peter Scott's pictures of them. On this occasion they appeared as a score of different pictures, each one coming to life before one's eyes and changing form, each with added beauty. Had it happened sooner I am almost doubtful if I could have brought my gun to my shoulder in the face of such a magnificent sight. By now in the increasing moonlight we were clearly visible and were soon left in the quiet of the night, alone, except for the barking of a farm dog that our shooting had disturbed. Then, of course, I almost fell over my bag!

At least it held the satisfaction of hot soup which, after collecting our birds, we dealt with in a summary manner. The total bag was only six geese and we felt very ashamed of our shooting, but if the fault of only six geese lay with us, at least there were those we should have killed able to return home alive to tell the tale also. That was the end of the season for me as the country became frostbound and all the inland birds were driven to the salt marshes and shore to make the best they could of it, and I was called away until after the season closed. This story has many lessons and morals and I hope that it may be of profit to other wildfowlers besides myself.

WILD FOWL SHOOTING AT HOLY ISLAND

By Sir Ralph Payne-Gallwey (1909)

I shot over the tidal flats for ten years, usually for six weeks after Christmas, with the assistance of one of the best puntsmen in England, with every appliance for obtaining sport, and at all hours by day and by night.

The Brent geese are seldom present in any number before Christmas, but after Christmas, and till the end of February, they are often very numerous. In a hard winter, especially if the weather is severe in North Holland and in Denmark, from 1500 to 2000 geese frequent the mudflats. In mild winters their numbers vary from 600 to 800. These birds are very difficult to obtain for the reason that they pass most of the day in security at sea, and only fly to the flats to feed on the sea grass (Zostera Marina) when the tide is low. They are then, as a rule, unapproachable, as they are careful to alight at a long distance from the water, and when a boat or punt can push up within a couple of hundred yards of them, on the flowing tide, they fly out to sea or to other parts of the flats where they are secure from the gunner.

At the same time, by the exercise of much patience, hard work night and day, and a good deal of luck, a shot at the Brent with a punt gun can now and then be achieved, especially in very windy weather, when they fly low and are not so apt to leave for a rough sea. But this only occurs when the wind is strong and, of course, on shore. In such favourable weather, and with plenty of frost, a bag of from 60 to 80 geese may be made during the month of January. I have obtained as many as 200 after Christmas, but with every exertion, as well as with good luck. The average number would seldom exceed eighty of these excessively wary fowl, and in mild winters perhaps not more than 40 to 50.

What causes all gunning afloat from Holy Island to be difficult is the fact that the entire estuary dries at low water, and that there are no creeks and channels along which a boat or duck punt can be paddled up to the birds as they rest or feed on the flats. If this was not the case the geese would not remain, as they would soon be driven away to other haunts. By anchoring a boat behind small promontories or under the shelter of rocks, occasional shots at the geese may be had with a shoulder gun as they fly from the sea to or from the mudflats, presuming always that the wind is strong enough to cause the birds to fly low.

As to other wildfowl there are very few. I have never seen a hundred wigeon together, and probably at most a couple of hundred frequent the flats, and then seldom during the daytime. In hard frost, wild duck are driven from inland ponds and rivers to the tide, and sometimes a score may be noticed, but usually not more than a half dozen here and there, and these are probably sleeping in safety on the dry ooze far beyond the reach of the fowler's gun. Teal are rare visitants; in ten years I scarce saw a dozen. Among diving ducks, the scaup is the common species at Holy Island, few others of this worthless tribe being seen. To an enthusiastic wild fowl shooter a fortnight at Holy Island in hard weather would be a delightful excursion, even if his bag were a relatively light one.

A NIGHT OF WILD FOWLING
IN THE NORTH KENT MARSHES

By W. Halliday (1909)

A hard blue sky is overhead, without a vestige of cloud; the wind blowing keen from the east, and the marshes covered with frozen snow, so deep in many places that few travellers would dare venture out there; but I want birds as specimens, and the long continued cold has made them tame.

The tide is running up and the birds are on flight from place to place. There are very treacherous traps for the unwary in the Saltings–that meadow-like space left between the salt water and the sea wall. To look at it you would think it easy travelling, but the thick growth of the sea blite and coarse grass and rush conceal the runs and dykes made by the rush of the tide, some of which lead to the sluice gates in the sea wall. The force of the tide opens these in flowing up, and fills all the dykes; when the ebb takes place the gates close again. Four, five, to eight feet in depth these runs and dykes are; only a marshman can go safely over these places.

Nothing is to be seen yet but a few hooded crows on the prowl. It is no use to think of shooting the saltings just now, so we turn into the marsh to look about for a bit; and the curlews screaming will let us know when the tide has turned. What a long dreary space it is, covered with glittering snow. But the cold is fearful, and a bird will not leave shelter if he can possibly help it; so we tramp on in the hope of a chance shot. Here and there we come upon the footprints of a heron, for the snow is soft round the margins of the springs. The other birds do not like him, for he is always hungry, and his stomach is very accommodating.

Near some pollard willows some starved-out fieldfares are bunched up. They utter a feeble "chuck" at times; their feathers are puffed out, making them look twice their natural size. A gull comes flapping over on the hunt, for a dead or wounded bird is a nice meal for him. From a bunch of dead flags with a "scape-scape-scape" up springs a snipe, with that twist and turn about flight peculiar to himself and his relatives. He is not fired at, for if there are any fowl in hiding anywhere in his line of flight that cry will move them.

It has done so. Three mallard rise from a dyke; they are low down, and fly straight to where I am standing by the willows; three in a line, their green heads glistening in the sun–for it is morning—and the red-brown of their breasts is showing distinctly. They are near enough now, I think—two of them, at any rate. "Bang!" "Quack, quack!" A twist and turn of their necks and bodies tells that they have been hit, but they do not fall. It serves one right, for it is almost useless firing at fowl coming right at you; the breast feathers are so thick. It is a warning to resist temptation for the future.

As we near the saltings, something springs from a patch of dead flag, which we shoot, and it proves to be a fine specimen of the Short Eared Owl or "woodcock owl" of the marshmen. His light body and hawk-like flight often lead folks to take him for some other bird. He hunts by day as well as in the evening; any hen-footed fowl is his prey - that is, if it is not too big for him. The shore shooters know him well; they see him, just as the light begins to fade, come skimming over the flats, now high up, the next moment close to the ground. All at once he stops, and fans with his wings, like a kestrel, over a tuft of rushes. That fanning of the wings is remarkable; it causes a current of air, much stronger than anyone would imagine, which rattles and stirs the dry rushes, so that any creature that has sheltered there comes out, and the owl gets it. His near relative, the long eared owl, has the same tactics. They do not eat all they catch at the time, but hide it till wanted, and the contents of their larder would surprise many people.

Gaining the foot of the sea wall, we crouch down for shelter, and listen for the notes of the fowl, driven by the fierce wind off the open sea to seek harbour in the bays. Then comes the screaming of the redshanks, the cackle of the gulls, and the cry of tern; all combined with the peculiar chatter of thousands of dunlins or "oxbirds." The fowl are coming up with the wind, so, crawling up the bank, we peep very cautiously out over the Saltings and down the creek. The whole place is alive with hen and web footed fowl. Only a mile away a line of birds is to be seen coming over from the opposite shore; we get quickly back to the bottom of the wall and wait for them.

The whistle of their wings is first heard, and then we can distinguish them. Wigeon they are, the feathers underneath shining like white satin. Picking out the leader as he passes by, and aiming a yard in front, we bring him down with a thud–dead. And now the fowl are on the Saltings; their scream, chatter, quack, and whistle, all mixed up together, while from the other side of the water comes the sound of the heavy duck guns hard at work.

We slip over the wall, and begin to crawl on hands and knees to the fowl feeding on the very edge of the ebb tide. Curlews are not to be thought of; they know exactly how far a gun will reach, and keep just the right distance out of harms way.

Besides, they post one of their number for sentry duty. The redshanks are nearly as bad, for they kick up a noise, and let all the other birds know that something is crawling along.

Getting under the shelter of the wall, I made my way lower down to the tide, where, crouching under the remains of a stack of reeds, I found a "shore shooter," one who makes his living by means of his gun. By some unlucky chance he had forgotten to fill his powder flask. The birds are well up on the Saltings, and he has only enough for another charge for his duck gun. Could I oblige him with a charge? He asked.

"Certainly, with half a dozen, if you like," is my reply.

"I can't afford to shoot them little hen footed things," he remarks. "Powder and shot cost money. Are you after something to stuff?"

"Well, yes; something in that way."

"Ah. I fancied you was by your shootin'. You let some fowl go by that I should have pulled at. You don't shoot for a livin'?"

"No, I do not."

"Shall you be down this part any more, think you?"

"Yes, I may, for anything I know."

"Well, there's some of your sort of birds about here, what

you're after, and I could knock a few over for you. Would this be any good to you? If it is, take it."

I was glad to have it, for it was a fine specimen of the Kentish Plover, or Dotterel—a rare bird even here.

"Can you live by your gun?" I asked.

"Sometimes; last winter I did well, though it was by chance like! It come about this way. I had to go to the marshes at the back of the island—Sheerness. You don't know it, do you?"

"I know it well, a shallow part especially, covered over with sea grass and weed, and a good nine miles from here."

"Ah, that's it! The geese are well sheltered there, with plenty of food, and they'd gathered from all parts. I brought home three couple on my first night, and sold 'em. Then I bought myself powder and shot, and a few other things, and went to work. Well, all through that winter I managed to live; rough work at times, mind you, but I lived, and that's somethin'. I allays keeps me own secrets. My line of work is shootin' fowl, an' I don't want anybody to help me!"

I gathered afterwards on the trudge home that my companion made a very good living indeed, though he made little noise and much less boast.

No one appears to have anything to say against the practice of shooting birds from the shore, or even with the shoulder gun on the stakes, but with the punt gunner it is totally different, if one may judge by the antagonism shown in the local press at times.

The sport of punting is variously summed up and condemned by those who do not possess a shooting punt. It is called murder, massacre, butchery, etc, the different degrees of nomenclature varying probably with the dislike, petty spite, or jealousy of the different critics.

The view which I have always held in relation to this matter is that undoubtedly punt shooting is one of the kings of sport, and it calls forth all the skill, patience, and energy requisite in a successful shore shooter, and a great deal more wariness and science are required in the punter, in his method of approaching his prey; therefore, why all this adverse criticism?

One can well imagine the exultation which necessarily fills the breast of the individual who has, with one discharge, captured a modest quarter of a hundred birds. Neither can I regard as inhuman punt shooting, for every precaution is taken, at all shoots, to kill, with the hand gun, all birds that have been winged or only slightly wounded.

AN OLD GUNNER AND HIS TWO SONS

THOUGHTS ON FLIGHTING

By B. St George

The behaviour of duck at the morning and evening flights is the greatest of all the fascinations of wildfowling. Judging when they will flight well and how the flight should be taken is a very difficult matter.

At first it all seems a question of luck. But gradually certain common denominators emerge from the successes and from the failures. Then the realisation dawns that success is not dependent upon the vagrant fancy of a lot of dilettante wildfowl but upon a host of factors which in reality are perfectly appreciable in advance. Some will incline the duck to flight early, some late, some to fly high, some to fly low; some to give up any idea of flighting at the conventional time; and finally some to leave the district altogether and vanish into thin air.

During the last three winters in North Germany I have returned home empty handed often. There is plenty of time during those long and weary walks home to consider failure and the reasons for it, and I cannot remember latterly an occasion when an explanation for failure has not suggested itself to me. I find now that I have unconsciously pieced together a pattern of the factors that affect the behaviour of duck at flight time which I believe will explain success or failure not only when shooting on estuaries such as the Elbe where much of my recent experience has been gained, but also on the open coast as well.

Initially I decided to take nothing for granted. After the first few totally inexplicable failures I even began to doubt that it was instinctive for duck to move at all at dawn and dusk. However, I am now convinced that this is so. I have not found that they will necessarily move seaward at dawn and inland at dusk. This is what they would like to do but other factors will often make them do otherwise. But whatever be the conditions, at these times they do become restless and take to the wing. I have watched even the tame ducks in London's parks behave in just this way, leaving their sanctuary at dusk to fly up the river and settle on mud flats or suburban reservoirs for the night.

The instinct to move in the morning and evening has been developed because basically ducks are water feeders (unlike many of the geese which like to feed on the land). They also like to feed by day, and prefer to do so in the safety of open water or wide mud flats. Hence they will, when they can, move out to sea at dawn and inland at dusk.

I have rarely had success in North Germany with the morning flight. The duck certainly move, and in general the direction is seaward. But flying into the daylight they have many hours in which to find and settle on to their feeding grounds and they are content to fly high and run no risks until they are well out over the open water. In the evening it is different. Though the duck has remarkable eyesight it does not have unlimited ability to see in the dark. At dusk duck are generally bound for small sheltered pools and ponds which they may not be able to locate once insufficient light remains to be reflected skywards off the surface of the water and so to guide them in. For this reason they like to flight in the evening before the light has gone whenever they can.

I believe there is truth in the theory that before the advent of the shotgun duck habitually flighted much earlier in the evening than they do today. It does not seem logical that the duck family should naturally seek out its night's resting place when it is nearly dark while all the other day feeders are settled for the night long before the light is gone. The outline of the pattern is, then, simple enough; duck will move at dawn and dusk; they feed by day and rest inland at night; in the evening they will try to settle before it is dark. But the detail of the pattern is more intricate. If it were not so, the shores of our estuaries would be lined with sportsmen every winter night and our larders would be full of mallard, teal and wigeon.

The first consideration is the effect of the weather. In estuary shooting particularly it is of great importance. In calm weather many of the duck will scatter over the open sea for the day and so the flight, when it comes, will be dispersed and unprofitable. In rough weather they will seek the sheltered waters of an estuary for feeding, collect there and so the flight inland at dusk will be concentrated. High winds or low visibility make them fly low. The ideal weather for the wildfowler is in fact the dirtiest. I would think twice before I ventured out at all to take the flight when the weather is calm and clear, but when the rain is being driven horizontally by half a gale I would try to summon up the courage to take not only the evening flight but the morning flight as well.

I believe too, that bad weather brings the duck inland off their feeding grounds earlier and so in better shooting light, and I am certain that heavy shooting in one area will frighten many birds into groping their way inland in the safety of darkness.

The effect of the moon is simply to make it easier for the duck to find its way to its night's rest. A good bright moon will therefore tend to postpone the flight time. Under such conditions duck will often continue to feed long after it is dark and the flight at dusk will not take place at all.

I have never found taking the flight at moonset successful. Many of the birds have already drifted inland in twos and threes before the moonlight begins to fade. In any event shooting under the moon is very chancy unless it is high and there is plenty of white fluffy cloud about to catch the moonlight and silhouette the birds. At moonset there is insufficient for this. There is nothing so exasperating as standing under a brilliant moon with duck hissing past ones ears but being unable to sight them unless by chance their silhouette actually pass across its face.

The ducks favourite feeding ground is the tideline. In estuaries and other shallow places where the tide moves in fast, the time of high tide has a very important effect on the flight. Duck will flutter in with the edge of the tide in short hops until it begins to reach the shore. They will then fly up and down the tideline looking for coves and beaches which may still be uncovered, where they may be able to feed for a little longer. On the Elbe estuary this tidal flight, which may only last for a dozen minutes, provides on occasions some of the best duck shooting in Europe.

When the tide pushes the duck off their feeding grounds just before dusk, it has a direct effect on the time of the flight. Once on the wing they do not consider it worth their while to settle on the open water for what remains of the day and will turn inland while the light is still good. Similarly they will flight late at low tide and may sometimes be content to spend the night on the shore if dusk coincides with the beginning of the ebb. In the latter case the evening flight may again not take place at all.

Next a word about the much vexed question of flight lines. Many is the time I have placed myself accurately on the shore at dusk confident that the arrow drawn on my map by some well wisher runs exactly through the blade of grass on which I am standing, and rarely can I remember it being any better than the stand I took up on the following night many hundreds of yards away.

My belief is that if the flight takes place while there is still enough light, the duck will cross the coast wherever they feel like crossing it. They will always tend to take short cuts across headlands and these are often good places to stand. On the other hand I do believe that the duck is guided when the light is poor by reflections off the water and that when flighting late they will tend to follow water courses. But I do not believe that there are mysterious invisible arterial skyways down which they throng nightly on their way inland, which bear no relation to landmarks or feeding grounds. Flight lines, like flight times, are related to conditions.

Finally, a word about the feeding grounds themselves. Although duck normally like to feed on the edge of the tide, if the land along the coast is wet and flooded into lakes and pools they will normally be tempted into deserting the sea shore and scattering inland for a change of diet. Where there is inland feeding aplenty particularly when the weather on the shore is stormy, many birds may well desert the sea altogether and under these conditions I would be chary of trying the flight at all. Conversely, when hard weather closes over the surface of all the inland pools and forces the duck back to the tideline for their food, the flights are generally good.

I have often amused myself by conjuring up in my mind the perfect combination of conditions for the evening flight. A wide shallow estuary, desolate and deserted, opens into the sea a mile or two to my right. It is late afternoon in mid-December, and the hinterland is gripped by a black frost. I am lying up at a place where a creek spills onto the mud in a dirty tortuous trickle.

A gale has been blowing from the North-East all day and there are flecks of snow in the wind. Many ducks have forsaken the open sea and gathered on the mud flats in front of me for shelter and food. The water in the creek beside me flows sluggishly inland with the fast rising tide and through binoculars I can see the duck wheeling and fluttering in small flocks as the tideline advances. The sky is overcast; it will be a dark moonless night. In a few moments now the tide will begin to cover the last feeding grounds and the duck will rise and move inland. The light begins to fade. . . . any minute now. . . . any minute now.

One day it will be a reality.

WILDFOWLING AFLOAT

By Walter H. Pope (1903)

I have previously discussed the fowler's shooting grounds and quarry and will now address myself to the fowler's equipment for the sport and the methods adopted for working his various appliances. It is, however, beyond the scope of this article to enter into minute details regarding the vexed question as to whether single or double handed punts are most suitable for fowling, as this depends very much on the nature of the particular locality and on the individual inclinations of the fowler, nor shall I dilate upon the various types of stanchion guns which may be used in the sport. There are, however, certain matters which require the fowler's careful consideration when fitting out for a shooting cruise, and I will offer a few practical suggestions which may be useful to him.

Stanchion guns are built in varying sizes, the weight usually corresponding to their size and power. There are the small light weapons weighing from 60lbs. to 75lbs., with a shot charge of from 8oz. to 12oz.; and there are also heavier guns made varying from 100lbs. up to 175lbs. and 200lbs. in weight, the largest of which would shoot 6oz. of powder and 2lbs. to 2.1/4 lbs. of shot. In a single handed punt I have known fowlers who use a comparatively heavy gun up to 130lbs. and 140lbs. in weight where fowl are numerous and a heavy shot now and again obtainable; but these large guns are likely to upset the trim of a single handed punt, unless the balance can be so regulated that the weight is evenly distributed without permitting the stock to come too far inboard and impede the fowler's movements.

For my single handed punt I used two muzzle loaders weighing respectively 75lbs. and 112lbs., and in my double punt a breech loader of 175lbs., firing a charge of 6oz. of powder and 2lbs. of shot. With the muzzle loaders I had two or three successful seasons in a single punt, and I have also found the larger of these guns quite suitable for a single handed punt. The great numbers of fowl, however, which I was in the habit of seeing at my fowling grounds abroad, ultimately necessitated the use of a double punt with the 175lbs. breech loader, and I found that this equipment answered admirably in every way.

In sheltered harbours, where birds are scarce and much persecuted by other gunners, a small gun from 60lbs. to 100lbs. in a light single punt will give capital results, and is quite capable of killing thirty or forty wigeon and even more at a shot if the chance occurs. The fowler, moreover, with a gun of this description would not hesitate to fire at half a dozen fowl, if no better shot was obtainable.

A small stanchion gun, however, would be totally inadequate for service in localities where wildfowl are abundant, as the fowler then requires a gun with greater range and spread when firing at large companies of birds. The punter who habitually fires long shots is the scourge of a fowling resort, and he does more to increase the shyness of the birds, and spoil the sport of the skilful gunner than might be imagined. Eighty yards is a fair range for a stanchion gun, though from 60 to 70 yards is better, and 50 better still. The true art of wildfowling consists of getting well up to the fowl, not pelting them with bullets at long range. A gun, therefore, which will carry its charge smartly and sweep the water at from 50 to 150 yards is all that is necessary for the most ambitious fowler.

Amateur fowlers generally prefer a breech loader, though as regards its shooting powers I think a strong well bored muzzle loader kills quite as well as the ordinary breech loaders. Much depends, of course, on the regular and even boring of the gun. A cylinder barrel is far more preferable to a choke bore, as it gives a wider and more even spread to the shot and will kill many more fowl. A friend of mine, an eminent authority on wildfowling, some time ago had an idea that a gun which could be built to shoot as close at 70 to 80 yards as the average cylinder does at 50 would be a decided improvement, for he had made extraordinary shot at fowl at close range when they were tightly packed and in a line in front of his gun. He argued, of course, that if such shots could be accomplished with a cylinder bore at 50 yards, similar results should be obtained with a slightly choked gun at 80 yards, which is about the ordinary range within which fowlers may often approach fowl. My friend, however, has not put his theories to the test, so I cannot say what might be done with a gun of that description.

Probably the best stanchion gun ever invented is the modern screw breech loader, which is safe and simple in mechanism, easily loaded, and water tight. Where geese and wigeon may sometimes be alternately the object of his stalk, it is a great convenience to be able to change the cartridge speedily, as two distinct sizes of shot are required for these fowl, and sometimes the fowler may have to change his cartridges several times a day–at least I have done so frequently. This is impossible, of course, with a muzzle loader, unless the fowler runs his punt ashore and unloads his charge every time he wishes to try for different kinds of fowl which necessitate a change of the shot.

And now as to the fowling punt. It is generally recognised that the punt should be suitable in every way to carry the gun, the punt and gun being, in fact, adapted to each other and the locality in which they are intended for service. A well built gunning punt should possess qualities of speed, buoyancy, ease in steering, and propulsion, and should be as low in the water when gun, crew, and gear are aboard as is consistent with safety. The lower she lies in the water and the more shapely her outlines, the less visible she will be to the fowl. Again, a long and moderately narrow punt is always faster, easier to propel, and holds her steerage way better in a wind than a short broad punt or a high sided punt.

The broad punt with the wind abeam frequently shows a tendency to fall away to leeward, whereas the narrower punt under such conditions, if the balance of the gun is properly adjusted, will turn her nose slightly up to the wind and facilitate propulsion. A perfectly equipped punt with its crew and gun should, in fact, take the water evenly from stem to stern, and the fowler can then work up to the birds in comparative ease and comfort. The dimensions and methods of construction of punts are given in most works on wildfowling, but those specified in Sir R. Payne-*Gallwey's Letters to Young Shooters* may be safely relied upon to satisfy the requirements of any fowler.

The punt's gear should comprise of the following articles: Hand paddles (for single handed punts), wooden set poles of two lengths, and a gun metal pronged set pole for punting over ice or sand. Oars, rowing spurs, gun rest, sculling crutch, ammunition box or bag, mud pattens for walking on soft oozes, shoulder gun, mast and small sprit sail, binoculars, and compass.

The stanchion gun rests along the foredeck balanced in a crutch attached to the centre of the face of the gunbeam, as the main beam of the foredeck is usually called. The muzzle is supported on the deck by a flat wooden gun rest with which the fowler raises or lowers the muzzle as may be necessary to aim at the birds. In adjusting the balance of the gun in the gun crutch, the muzzle should have an overbalance of about 8lbs. as it lies on the rest, so that when firing at birds the gun remains steady.

The recoil of the gun is usually absorbed by a rope breeching, roved through a hole in the stem block of the punt and looped with a spliced loop round the trunnions of the gun. This is safest and most simple way of easing the recoil, and the gun throws the charge more accurately and smartly than with any other device.

The punt and stanchion gun, with the various fittings, being now ready for sea, the next question that arises is how the punt may be best worked when stalking fowl in the open on the shallows and also in deep water. Broadly speaking, the art of punting consists in the fowler's ability, firstly, while lying concealed on the floor of his punt, to stealthily and noiselessly propel her within gunshot of a company of fowl on water or mud; and secondly, to so accurately judge his distance, aim and fire his gun as to bag the largest number of them, whether there be many or few birds to shot at.

In a single handed punt the fowler lies face downwards at full length, with his feet well under the afterdeck and his chest supported by a cushion, or perhaps a coat. Extending his arms through the openings in the wash boards, he then propels the punt with short hand paddles, one in each hand, by working them to and fro under water. When punting over the shallows he turns his paddle edgeways to the mud, and pushes the punt along until he draws within range of his birds. Then dropping his paddles, which are secured by cords to holes in the wash boards, places his hand on the stock of his gun, takes aim, and fires. This is the system adopted by professional fowlers on the east coast of England, but I have never seen it in practice on the southern estuaries or harbours.

During a long stalk in cold weather the fowler's hands sometimes become numbed when in perpetual contact with sea water, and there is, too, the risk, after dropping the paddles, that the punt may drift away with the wind from the direction of the fowl and thus expose him broadside to their eyes. Personally, I have never "set" a punt up to birds in this way, as I have always found it quite easy to push her over the shallows with the "set pole" when lying flat on my chest and with my arms stretched through the open wash boards, keeping it low down, well out of sight, and close to the surface of the water in taking each stroke. In the deep water and channels, by lying on my left side and sculling an oar in the starboard sculling crutch, the punt can also be easily propelled.

There are other methods too of working the punt, for some fowlers paddle a double handed punt when lying on their backs at the bottom of the punt, with their heads resting on the fore part of the afterdeck. I have not tried this method, but in Holland, I understand, it is a common practice among fowlers. The secret of working the punt is to lie low, conceal every movement of the arms and shoulders as far as possible, and avoid all noise when going into birds, whilst, of course, carefully keeping the punt's head "dead on" to the fowl all the time. When sculling, perhaps, for half an hour against wind and tide, the fowler may feel the strain on his wrists and arms, but this disappears after a little practice when the muscles have become accustomed to the work.

However skilfully the fowler may manoeuvre his punt, if he be unpracticed in the methods of setting, aiming, and firing his gun, all his skill in stalking will be unavailing. Few fowlers can fire such an unwieldy weapon as a stanchion gun from hand without the assistance of a gun rest, and it is therefore, usual before approaching birds to "set" the gun at a certain elevation by lowering or raising the muzzle to a certain height, so that the shot will sweep everything before it at from 40 to over 100 yards range. To do this the fowler lies down in his punt and takes a full sight at some object on the shore, say at from 70 to 80 yards distance–which is an average range for shooting fowl–and marks the handle of the gun rest with a notch, which indicates the exact position in which it should be for shooting.

Then, when stalking these birds, if the sight bears on their heads he knows that he is within killing range. There is considerable difficulty, however, in judging distance accurately, when one is lying prone at the bottom of the punt. Generally birds look much nearer on the water or mud than they really are, and when the excitement is at its highest pitch, at 100 yards they may often seem 30 or 40 yards closer. Correct distance judgment can only be acquired by long practice, but if the sexes of the birds, their bright eyes, or the colouring of their feathers and the outlines of their wings and tails can be clearly distinguished, it is considered a fair indication that the birds are in shot. In taking a somewhat longer shot than usual, errors of judgment occur, more especially when a bright sun is shining, which is a most deceiving light in which to estimate distance.

When approaching birds in position on ooze or water, the fowler should quickly decide as to how he will shoot at them, whether sitting or flying. His actions must be prompt and deliberate at that moment, for any hesitation would be fatal to success. There is, of course, less risk of missing a sitting shot if the fowl are stationary, and neither they nor the punt bobbing about in the water. At any distance up to 70 yards the gun should be aimed at the heads of the middle birds of the pack when they are extended in a line or in a compact mass, and the lower pellets will kill the nearest birds as well.

A charge of shot from a stanchion gun, however, nicely scattered among a pack of wigeon just as they spring aloft, will be far more effective, and will kill many more birds than if fired at them sitting, because every pellet has its billet, and but few are wasted. A flying shot, however, necessitates very accurate timing and a correct elevation of the gun. Should the trigger be pulled one second too late, the result may be a clean miss or, at most, the killing of one or two of the tail birds, which spring last of all.

In shooting geese and other slow rising fowl, it is best to fire at them about 6 or 8 feet up in the air, and if they spring in a cluster, the target is far larger and thicker. I have shot some thousands of brent with a stanchion gun, but only very occasionally have I fired at them sitting. One day, however, when stalking about five hundred of these birds which lined the outside edge of some ooze banks whilst feeding, I could not resist the temptation of shooting at them as they sat. In front of me I saw a veritable forest of heads and long necks in a thick line, as they stood and gazed at me within about 50 yards range, presenting thus an ideal shot for a punt gun. In this case I do not think I could have done better had I taken a flying shot, for I laid low forty three of these grand fowl, of which thirty three were killed on the spot.

In loppy water when the punt is dancing about on the wavelets, it is generally best to shoot as the fowl rise from the water or mud, otherwise, if fired at them when sitting, the shot may be entrapped by the waves, and the fowler will fail to score. A flying shot indeed should always be a "snap" shot at from 6 to 8 feet in the air, for after attaining this height the birds at once begin to separate to gain wing room for themselves.

A sitting shot on the water or mud must be made just as the fowls raise their heads and are in the act of stretching their necks to fly. Through the smoke of the gun after firing it often happens that the fowler can observe birds dropping out of the pack. Most of these will have been fatally struck when they had already sprung. Nothing but constant practice, however, and careful attention to the movements and positions of the fowl when stalking them, can make the fowler perfect in taking the fullest advantage of his opportunities. Every punter must remember instances of dismal failures, when he has clean missed the birds by shooting over them, or possibly shot too late, and I think it very unlikely that these features will ever disappear from the many hazards of the sport.

In hard winters fowl often visit the tidal bays and estuaries in vast numbers, and I have once or twice in my life seen the flats of my fowling quarters abroad simply swarming with geese, wigeon, ducks, teal, and all kinds of fowl. To give some idea of what sport the fowler may have when ice and snow have invaded the haunts of fowl, I have extracted the following notes from my diary for the season 1892 - 1893:-

December 31, 1892–Day fine; bitter wind from east. Mud frozen up and huge packs of ice floes close along shore. Out before low water. Masses of duck, teal, geese, wigeon, and pochard here and there seeking shelter under the ooze banks from the heavy wind. "Set" down to a fine lot of ducks, but not being well together, gave them up. Large pack of wigeon stretched out along the line of the main channel tempted us; got to about 70 yards and fired, amassing 38. Sea very rough for gathering cripples. Night too rough for shooting.

January 1, 1893.–Afloat at dawn on the ebb. Large quantity of ice lying close in shore, but we could not get through. Strong breeze from east. Day fine and bright. Masses of birds everywhere. Through lack of water and constant struggles with ice floes, too late for a shot at a big pack of wigeon, but by making a detour later, fired and bagged 28. On the flood tide shot at a small bunch of ducks and bagged 12. calm all night. Moon one day off the full. Afloat at 7 o'clock. Fired at a fine company of wigeon 200 yards to windward of some small patches of rocks and bagged 51. Home and in bed 11 o'clock. Bag for day 89.

January 2.–hard frost all night; morning quite calm. Afloat on the ebb, 8.30. Owing to arrival of fishing boats in our bay, determined to try a large bay two miles down the gulf. Went ashore on the island there. A large company of wigeon close in on the flats under the shore of another island. Set down, with the gun astern, and bagged 49. On the way home fell in with another lot of wigeon, fired, and retrieved 29, nearly half we shot at. In many instances today fowl were sitting on the ice, and we could not have gathered them had we succeeded in killing any, for the ice was too thin to bear one's weight and too thick to force the punt through. Bag 78.

January 4.–Dead calm after hoar frost; weather bright and sunny. Afloat at 10.30. Fishing boats disturbing fowl. Got 30 wigeon and a mallard for a water shot when birds were adrift at high tide. Subsequently rowed over to a big bay below. Masses of wigeon and brent on the edge of the flats. Waited for low water. Set to the fowl. Geese sprang up without driving away the wigeon. Fired and bagged 74 wigeon. Night unpropitious. Bag for day 104.

January 5.–When firing at wigeon yesterday, punt evidently ashore.

January 6.–Stern block broken with recoil of gun. Punt under repairs.

January 7.–Afloat again. Strong wind from S.E.' barometer falling; ice giving. Tried the ducks, but they were again too scattered for a shot. Got two small shots at wigeon of 24 and

21 respectively. Bag for day 45.

January 8.–Heavy rain all night. Ice giving; wind S.S.E. moderate. Plenty of fowl about. Setting to a big pack of wigeon, when a gull dashed down and drove them up. Shot from a fishing boat drove up a big lot of wigeon which came subsequently and pitched on muds near us. Set down under cover of twilight and bagged 70 of them. Home at 7 p.m.

During this season of 1892–93 sport was exceptionally good, although the hard frost experienced in December and January did not last long. According to my diary, the total bag amounted to 2061 birds of which 630 were brent geese, 1307 wigeon, 40 wild duck, 1 teal, 1 pochard and "various." The heaviest shot at geese realised 43, the two best at wigeon 89 and 85 respectively, besides ten others exceeding 50 birds per shot.

Although ill luck may, perhaps, attend the fowler's efforts by day, he has always a chance of retrieving his fortune by night, provided that the conditions are favourable for punting. If there are many fowl in the locality, they will certainly be on the oozes at night, for that is the time when the wigeon and ducks chiefly feed, though, should they be unmolested, they often do so by day. Under cover of the darkness the wildest fowl are usually more accessible than in daylight, and the fowler can then steal upon them unseen and unsuspected.

Soon after dusk "trip" after trip of wigeon, duck and other fowl may be heard passing overhead from their diurnal resort on the coast to their favourite banks of ooze in the bays. At intervals, larger groups of fowl sweep over the darkening skies, uttering their cheery notes as they view once again below them their beloved haunts, and finally the main army arrives, and a continuous stream of birds may be heard rushing through the air for several minutes. A few small parties of late flying birds then bring up the rear.

The time of flight in certain localities is subject to some modification, and on bright clear nights I have often heard birds flighting as late as 9 o'clock. On arrival at their feeding grounds the wigeon at once commence feeding if the mud banks are uncovered, but as a rule they do not congregate in large numbers so early in the night. Wild ducks and teal generally feed by night in the vicinity of fresh water, if possible, and sit tucked away in the shady corners of the smaller bays until daylight appears. One of the chief difficulties which the fowler has to contend with at night lies in finding his birds and in locating their exact position. Generally speaking, he is first attracted to the spot where the fowl are feeding by their cries, which are audible at a considerable distance on calm nights.

Wigeon and duck are often noisy and loquacious when about to begin their meals, and also when the rising tide commences to flood their feeding grounds and they collect over the high patches of mud to get the last mouthful of food. A trained ear, and an accurate knowledge of their haunts and habits, is thus an absolute necessity for the night punter, and he must ever be on the alert, for sometimes the faintest cry, or even the splashing of a single bird, may convey information of the utmost importance to his success. At times, too, wigeon and duck speak so little during the night that their whereabouts can only be discovered by the dabbling noises which they create with their bills when feeding on the sloppy ooze banks, to hear which the fowler must generally be lying within but a short distance of his quarry. I have observed that fowl are also exceptionally silent on very bright calm moonlight nights. I suppose that they can see and are in touch with each other, so that there is no reason for them to be calling so often. On nights, too, when a hoar frost is falling, and everything seems supernaturally calm and quiet, fowl are restless as well as silent, only at odd intervals giving any sign of their presence.

The fowler may have some doubts, when wigeon are not

loquaciously disposed, and he cannot see them under the moon, whether there are few or many birds in the company which he intends to stalk. A shrill, long-drawn note–"threeel"– is the cry of the cock wigeon, and if often repeated indicates that he has but few comrades with him. The note of the hen is a kind of growl or "purre," and when frequently heard in conjunction with the more sibilant cries of the cock bird, it may be taken for granted that the company is a large one. Eventually, if he listens attentively, the wigeon will break out in a "chorus," and his doubts will the be set at rest. When stalking them, however, should their suspicions in any way be aroused, they suddenly become silent; but if the chorus of voices commences again, the fowler may confidently push in for his shot.

Favourable nights for punting are those when there is a half or three quarter moon, low down and late, with a slight ripple on the water. A full moon high overhead on a calm night usually gives too much light, and the surroundings are too clearly visible for the fowler to work up to his birds under propitious conditions, though, with a dark ripple astern of him, his chances would be improved. Under a big moon there is practically no shade from which he can advance on his quarry, and his punt can easily be discerned by them at some distance. When the full moon is clouded over, however, this is often the very best opportunity for stalking birds at night, for the light is then evenly distributed all around, and he can choose any direction which suits him best for advancing to the attack.

On bright starlight nights too, when there is no moon and the horizon is clear and without haze, he may approach fowl closer perhaps than at any other time. I can recall to mind many occasions when I could certainly have almost touched birds had I been disposed to do so. Colonel Hawker says that bright starlight is the very best of all times for getting at birds, as the tide flows over the mud, and particularly if there is a slight breeze without wind enough to blacken the shallows. On the "ground ebb" the shallows become quite white, and the birds are easily distinguishable. The same effect is produced also on the flood tide when the water flows over the mudbanks. Under the moonbeams birds are often visible on the water far away, and the fowler finds no difficulty in stalking them under those conditions. During foggy, hazy, or dark nights, however, it is useless to go afloat after fowl, as, in addition to the possibility of losing oneself in the darkness, there is also the chance of being left high and dry on the oozes if the tide is ebbing.

I have one or two dire and dismal reminiscences of having passed the night out in a fog shivering in my punt, awaiting the flood tide to come and release me from my unfortunate position, and on one occasion, whilst fowling in a locality which was new to me, I was clad in only a light dinner suit and slippers when I went afloat! This experience was due to the temerity of a friend who was dining aboard the fowling sloop with me, and was anxious to have his first experience in wild fowl shooting. We were on the deck after dinner, and hearing a large company of wigeon yelling like demons seemingly close to us, we put off in the punt to try them. As it turned out. However, the fowl were actually a long way in shore, and by the time we reached them and had fired our shot a fog settled over the water, hid everything from view, and we were lost!

There are dangers too in night shooting, especially in localities where fowlers are numerous. Once I was covered by the gun of a fowler who was actually "setting up" to the same pack of wigeon which I was engaged in stalking from the opposite direction under the shade of the shore. Evidently he had not the remotest notion of my propinquity, though I could see him plainly in his punt. As he drew near I startled him by shouting in alarm, and he told me subsequently what a fright I had given him. I need hardly say that it was mutual! The rules for night punting do not differ materially from those which apply to day punting, for of course the fowler should take advantage when stalking birds of every little circumstance which may tell in his favour. He must always work his punt from the shade or from some background towards the light, and be cautious in making no sound which might tend to alarm the fowl, as they are quite as alert in hearing as in seeing.

Although no doubt fowling by night is a somewhat lonely and fatiguing pursuit, and moreover often a very cold one, it is under the moon and stars that the fowler may often get a good bag of birds, and he has then the best chance of studying their habits and demeanors under the most favourable and exciting conditions. The fascination of the sport is no doubt difficult to understand for those whose minds dwell on the cold, the stress of the weather, and the occasional blanks that have to be endured, but the interest and excitement are so keen that such drawbacks are soon forgotten; and if any man persists in doubting that the sport has its attractions, I would only say to him, "Try it."

THE SPORTING COOT

By A. Johnson

I found the reed fringed lake when I was fishing for carp in the summer, and I made up my mind to return to it in the winter for it was a coot haunt. It was one of those beautiful narrow strips of water common in Suffolk and had once been used no doubt as a duck decoy–a secretive place where every rustle and sound in the reeds and withies denoted bird and animal life.

There are few water loving birds more crafty or cunning than "bald headed" coots. Knowing this, I began to stalk cautiously fifty yards before I reached the edge of the rushes that provided me with plenty of cover. As I sat in hiding, the stink of rotting and waterlogged vegetation was pungent and filled my nostrils but it is not unpleasant to those who like watery places–the haunts of duck, wigeon, teal and herons. There is something bitter sweet yet rich about the smell of a reed fringed pool that is hard to describe.

Very soon I spotted the coots–black dots in clear silhouette on the water's surface–but they were spread out all over the lake. Unlike other wild fowl coots do not pack on the water; they are far too clever to become vulnerable in this way. The only time one sees coots together in anything like close formation is when they are on the wing or when they gather to feed on the ooze where the reeds have been cut or rotted away. But even at flighting time coots are deceptive and are never as dense as they appear at a close distance, and never as tight in a pack as wigeon.

Though in habit and appearance coots are not unlike large moorhens, they have a distinctive flight. They fly considerably faster than moorhens with their heads straight out and their legs hanging down. I believe that this is done in an effort to counterbalance the centre of gravity which is not well placed– the wings of a coot are too far forward and near to the neck. The moorhen has something of the same difficulty but it manages to carry its head erect when on the wing.

All the birds before me on the mere remained out of range, though there was a slight drift on the water in my direction and I hoped that they might be floated gradually towards me. This, however, was not the case. Every few minutes the coots paddled fast against the run of the water, keeping a safe distance, and seemingly always at a fixed distance between each bird. I was beginning to think it was hopeless when I heard several coot calls–like the clicking of stones struck together– and without any apparent reason the birds began to gather in a pack. Hardly believing my good fortune, they swam quickly towards the bank where I was in close hiding. . . . a black fleet of birds with their white pates catching the sun.

It was then that I looked up and saw a buzzard circling overhead, eying the coots below with great interest, turning its head this way and that as if to get a better view. I believe my position had been spotted by the hunter in the sky, and that the coots were being deliberately herded towards me with the object of a kill being made when they scattered in wild confusion. The packing of the coots did not make them more vulnerable to attack, for their numbers were far too formidable for a chicken hearted buzzard.

A moment later I got in two easy shots as the birds rose with a rush of wings, flinging up foam and making a loud clanking noise. As I had expected, the buzzard shot down, taking advantage of the coots' confusion, and it disappeared from view in close pursuit over the reeds. After this encounter with coots I came to take a close interest in the birds wherever I came across them on the meres of the district.

The best way to get at coots is in a punt, but even so they are not an easy quarry and the excitement of the difficult approach is intense. Like pochards, coots will swim away from a punt, preferring to trust their legs rather than their wings. They make for the concealing reed beds and play an expert and eccentric game of hide and seek with the fowler. The birds pop in and out of the water, creep along the bank as fast as a water vole, run over the ooze. . . . in fact they do anything but take to wing. If the birds can be forced up, they make good shooting and they fly wilder and higher each time they leave the water. The fowler has one advantage at least where coots are concerned. When once the birds have adopted a haunt it takes a great deal of shooting to drive them away to another water or mere, even though a suitable one is quite near at hand.

In many ways coots are like duck and they are often seen on decoys in company with them. There are, however, marked differences and in some respects their habits are the exact reverse of other wildfowl. Coots, for instance, feed by day and roost by night in the reeds and rushes surrounding their haunts. A wounded duck or wigeon always makes for water but a winged coot immediately makes for the cover of reeds and eludes pursuit by swimming and diving close in shore. Even in the hands of a fowler, a wounded bird shows great tenacity of life and care should be taken in the handling of a wounded bird, for it is capable of inflicting a nasty gash with its talons.

Duck and wigeon like the company of coots–perhaps they come to rely on the inordinate caution of these birds. As wildfowl often sleep in the daytime and coots are feeding in the daylight, carefully guarded by "watch-out" birds, the partnership is obviously advantageous to duck and like species. I have observed that resting mallard are far more suspicious when coots are also present on a feeding site or decoy, but what the fowler loses on the swings he may well gain on the roundabouts, for coots make excellent decoys in themselves. Other flighting fowl see them easily and drop to them. From the decoy keeper's point of view, however, the balance is against the coots and they are always considered vermin. They will eat any "planted" grain and they will also destructively tear up valuable wigeon grass, which is often scarce enough.

It is fairly easy to pick out coots on the water from other wildfowl. Apart from their scattered formation, the birds always carry their heads low, as if intently listening, and thrown forward in a poking attitude. When swimming, the tail sticks up high behind and well out of the water.

Only when inland waters become ice covered in the winter

do coots take themselves off to the estuaries, where they can feed easily on the more open brackish waters and along the foreshore. I have heard it said that they particularly like to nibble at the white crusty froth left by an ebbing tide. Old fowlers once collected this scum and put it near lakes and ponds to attract the birds to new feeding sites. If the weather is rough along the sea coast, coots will at once seek their old haunts and shelter inland. But even in soft weather one may sometimes find old male birds haunting the estuaries and creeks; I believe that these birds remain throughout the year. Though tenacious of life, and birds that take a lot of shot, there are far fewer coots than there were fifty years ago. Perhaps no bird has suffered more in fen areas on account of the draining and reclamation of the meres and bogs for agricultural purposes.

They were once considered better eating than duck and sold by the thousand to London poulterers and dealers. Coots make good eating provided one has the patience and time to dress and cook them properly. The body is covered beneath the feathers in a fine, closely adhering down, and it can only be got off by continual rubbing with a piece of resin. If, as is often the case, the hasty cook skins the bird, much of the gamey flavour is lost and the carcass dries out in the oven unless frequently basted.

Another way to deal with coot in the kitchen is to skin them, soak the breasts in weak salt water, and make into a pie. It is worth knowing that those birds shot in the morning before they have fed have always the best flavour. Not long ago I was talking to an old fowler just short of 100 years old who attributed his longevity to "the eating of coots and little else" as a young man.

A KEEN SPORTSMAN STILL.

A SNIPE CENTURY

By "Conrad"

I was camped at Balishah in the Larkana District of Sind when a local Zemindar invited me to shoot snipe on his land. His last instructions were to bring three hundred cartridges. To my inquiry if there would be any duck, he replied: "There is no hope." So I added fifty No. 5's to the ammunition.

I left camp at 8.30 a.m. and took the wherewithal for a snack during the day–sandwiches, cake, fruit and soda water, decanted into thermos flasks in the cool of the morning when the temperature was about 40 degrees Fahrenheit. A bottle of beer to finish the day was not forgotten, and my shooting seat, game carrier, cigarettes for myself and beaters completed the outfit. A little chat with my host, mutual agreement that it was an ideal day for a shoot–a light breeze, a clear sky and neither too hot for the heavy walking nor too cold to make the birds restive–then recognition of the head shikari and some of the beaters as old friends and off we went.

It was just ten o'clock when I reached my first stand. I had realised when in this area before that it was no place for walking up birds, varying depths of water surrounding small mounds of hard earth from which one slipped, at the critical moment into mud a foot or more in depth. The ground was nicely divided by small embankments and I decided to have the compartments driven towards me.

The head shikari, who had elected to come with me, and direct operations from the flank, had a voice like a foghorn and at every blast a wisp of snipe rose. As the instructions were repeated by the beaters in the distance, in equally stentorian voices, there were quite a number of birds on the wing before the beat ever began. The few which came near me caught me rather unsettled and the first beat was not a very promising start as the pick-up was only two!

A little advice to the assembled company on the effect of the human voice on all game birds improved matters and the next beat was more productive. I finally finished this patch of about forty acres in the first hour with twenty three birds on my carrier. The majority were "Jack," the full snipe flying very wide. We next crossed a high embankment to a large area of flooded ground about three furlongs away and while going to my position with reeds on either side, about ten white-eye pochard rose. I was loaded with "nines" but they were so close that one crumpled up to my first barrel and the second fell in thick reeds too far away to give any hope of recovery. These shots put up quite a number of duck, chiefly white-eye, teal and a few mallard. A good bunch of white-eye came over and one was added to the bag.

This spot was full of snipe and the first drive added seven to the bag, the best result of any beat so far. The going here was more difficult, especially as I had to leave the embankment and wade out one hundred yards to the cover of some tamarisk bushes. There were quite a number of duck on the wing all the time and an unsuspecting teal came too close with fatal results. The snipe were nearly all "full" and often rose in wisps of a dozen or more. The bag was increasing and the game carrier more than full. The picking up was decidedly good and it was seldom that a bird was not found. At the end of a drive I could tell the beaters the number of birds down and the approximate position of most of them. It was most noticeable how they fell in certain areas on either side of me which, I think, indicates that we all have our favourite angle for taking birds, and I certainly had plenty of choice as the birds came at all distances and angles.

It was now nearing one o'clock and I was ready for my lunch, but the beaters had seen a couple of mallard settle in a small patch of cover which had not been included in the last drive, so we decided to try for them. Thinking there were no more duck, I continued attending to the snipe, when the unforeseen happened. Up got another drake mallard and although he was none too near, a dose of nines, well in the neck, was too much for him. And so to lunch with a bag of seventy five snipe and five duck. It being the month of Ramzan, the beaters, all Mahamedans, were keeping the Roza, fasting between sunrise and sunset. This did not prevent them enjoying cigarettes which they smoked by holding them between the third and fourth fingers, making a bowl of the two hands and drawing the smoke through a hole between the thumbs; after a few puffs the cigarette was passed on to the next man. They are very cheery fellows. The wag of the party, on this occasion, was an old man of some seventy summers with a red beard, who entertained us with a demonstration of how to shoot, collapsing in a heap to represent a kill for every imaginary shot. My suggestion that his method was probably to get a good crowd of birds on the ground, creep up to them and fire into the middle, caused some amusement and, I suspect, was very near the truth.

How often the break for lunch upsets one's shooting! This day was no exception. The drives were across open fields with no cover, a strong breeze had blown up and the snipe were coming like streaks. Not only were they coming at a great pace, but they were mixed up with other non-sporting birds of the wading variety, and it was difficult. The "full" snipe zigged and zagged just when I fired, the Jack without any warning, would decide to alight just when I had pressed the trigger and a bird which had fallen would find he was only stunned and elect to regain consciousness and fly off when a beater went to retrieve him.

Thus it was I had three very bad drives and my stock of nines was getting low. I had some sevens in reserve but I always have the feeling that they are just too big for good snipe shooting. The fourth drive, however, produced better results and I had an idea I had just about reached the century. A count up found it to be one hundred and three. I decided this was enough, but seeing a few duck rising from the reeds the head shikari suggested a final beat for them. I took up my position at the end of the reeds and the shikari went out on the flank to stand in the open in an endeavor to direct the birds over me. In going out he must have put up a dozen mallard. A couple came over rather high on which I wasted two shots and then went on to bag a couple more snipe to end the day.

We changed and counted the bag. One hundred and five snipe of which eighty were full snipe and twenty five Jack, plus thirteen assorted duck. Cartridges used—two hundred and twenty one in five and a half hours shooting.

THIS WILDFOWLING FEVER

By Coombe Richards

What, one wonders, is the make-up of a 'fowler? It must, I think, be something in the blood, perhaps something elemental handed down–even though it may lie dormant for a generation or more–which eventually comes to the surface and produces that strangely alluring call with which all wildfowlers are familiar. To most it comes in youth, but I have known men to be first bitten with it when getting on for middle age and, I believe, once the addiction comes–for, like salmon fishing, that is what it amounts to–it remains until we are too old and feeble to carry on; and even then I suspect strongly a sense of the nostalgic lingers when the moon is right and tides suit.

I caught my first dose of wildfowling fever as a boy when accompanying my father and an old professional in the then wilder reaches of Poole Harbour. The tang of wet mud, the whine of wind across the saltings, the loneliness, the multitude of different bird voices bit deep into my young being and a love of them was born which, thank God, still burns brightly.

That first trip was but the beginning; every hour of it was precious as I listened enthralled to the conversation, went out–but not always–with my elders; became familiar with duck punts, ropes, stockholm tar and all the paraphernalia and exciting preparations for flighting or stalking. I learnt the glory of a sunset or of a wild tempestuous dawn, and the thrilling whicker of wings overhead when fowl are on the move. The never to be forgotten sense of pride and achievement when the little 20 bore smashed down my first duck; a fat mallard over which, in secret, I had a desire to weep!

Since that long ago expedition the quest for duck and geese has taken me far and wide, in fine weather and foul; mostly the latter, and I have loved every moment of it, although–and I confess it quite candidly–I have yet to experience one of those real red letter days about which we sometimes read. My' fowling has, more often than not, been remarkable only for the lightness of the bag, and for the wetness and discomfort endured during long hours of waiting and hoping. 'Fowling is like that, except perhaps for a fortunate few, yet that, of course, is all part of its appeal. It is a tough, uncertain job, the rewards of which are usually more than well earned.

Casting memory back across some forty years at the game, certain instances and mind-pictures remain fresh and distinct; little gems sparkling brightly. For instance:-

Dusk and a sou'-westerley gale blowing in over a desolate coastline, and five gunners running out of cartridges one evening flight, for we had not expected much. Birds killed against the grey, torn sky as they came over the seawall with the wind under their tails, hurtling away behind like cricket balls hit for six; and one solitary right and left, the memory of which will always bring a glow.

A wigeon flight from a clump of gorse bushes halfway down a cliff face in an Irish estuary; following upon a day spent chasing grey lag geese and three in the boat at the end of it.

Not least of that outing's enjoyment was the company of an old local 'fowler–whose gun I would not have fired for a fortune–but whose knowledge of the ways and habits of our quarry was unrivalled.

A rustling reed bed on the Hampshire coast and springs of teal coming and going all day–mostly too fast to be coped with successfully but heavy on cartridges, and a spaniel making some glorious retrieves.

Thirteen hours in a gun punt on the Wash, commencing at 3 a.m. in a snow blizzard and ending in torrential rain and a nor'-easterly gale. The gun had been fired only twice in all that while—for little reward; but the sights and sounds of that outing are indelible, although one has long forgotten the time it took to thaw out and get dry.

Punt gunning is not, of course, every wildfowler's choice and I doubt if today there are anything like as many punts afloat (including those handled by professions) as there were even before the war; it is a fascinating if dying side of the sport. Let us look at a typical day. . . .

We set off down some estuarine creek long before daylight, wondering what sort of fools we are to be out of bed at that hour, let alone being afloat, muffled in sweaters, duffle coatss and sea boots, nosing our way into an ice laden wind and the threat of worse to come. Soon, however, such thoughts are forgotten; the water slaps against the bows, the tide seeps and whispers across the mud flats. Far off a channel buoy winks its warning to coast-wise shipping. A startled waterfowl, disturbed in its solitude, rises shrieking but unseen in the darkness. The creak of the oars in the rowlocks, an occasional grunt from one's companion, sucking his pipe in the stern. All this has its appeal, and later, when the first silver streak heralding the dawn flickers along the eastern horizon, one realises that it is worth the trouble. What matter if the rain lashes down: the worse the weather, possibly the better our chances, for bad visibility and rough water help to hide our movements.

And then, lurid, angry and yellow, the sun rises behind the wind torn scudding clouds, showing itself momentarily. The oars have been abandoned, both of us are lying now on our bellies–and a gun punt in bad weather is no feather bed–one at the gun and the other at the paddles or quant. Only the tops of our heads peer over the weather boards, scanning with anxious eyes the scene around us. Fowl are all over the place, little parties moving hither and thither–and there, a quarter of a mile distant, is a dark patch on the water; is it brent, wigeon, mallard, or only a company of gulls?

We set up to it, maneuvering to keep down wind, slithering along, a grey white shadow in the welter of grey water and spume. Ten minutes later we alter course and make for another gathering of birds, for that first lot had been gulls and of no interest to us. These we discover are wigeon, the wariest of duck; we literally hold our breaths as yard by yard we creep nearer and nearer. With a cross wind and tide and a mud bank under our lee this is no easy matter, but at last there remains only ten yards to go—and that sometimes might just as well be miles, for an out of range shot is not to be considered; one must be within killing distance before the birds jump.

This little company seems less alert than is usual, and almost before we realise it we are there in precisely the right spot. To be too close cuts down the shot spread. Kicking hard on the bottom boards to give the alarm, he at the gun has his left hand on the butt and his right gripping the lanyard, whilst the punt itself is brought to bear on the target.

Wooosh! With a thunder of wings they are up and away almost as one bird. The toggle is pulled, the gun belches and roars. It was a reasonable shot, all things considered, but might have been better. Seven dead birds lie on the water and three winged ones flounder nearby; the latter to be dispatched with a cripple stopper snatched from its slings under the decking.

An hour later we get a shot at some brent and then it is all over, for the tide is too low and until it flows once again there is only gutter crawling to fill in the time. Three curlew, a mallard and a couple of 'shank are our reward for this.

We are cold and wet when at last course is set back for home, the making tide now lapping the "muds" and deepening the channels. Another shot, this time at mallard, is assayed on the way in, but is bungled and we gather only two birds. The sun has set, still wicked and glaring, as we row up the creek and haul the punt out, but our work is by no means completed. The gun must be un-shipped and thoroughly cleaned, and all our gear cared for and stowed; and then the long drive inland through the dark.

This wildfowling fever is a pleasant disease, it gives one solitude and has so many compensations. The dawns and the dusks, the lonely places, the company of lovely wild birds. The sad voice of the curlew, the trill of a whimbrel, the shriek of the redshank, the clamour of geese. The twisting, silvery flight of dunlin, knot and the other small tribes; the stare of an old seal out on the banks. The smell of the tideway, whine of wind and whisper of water.

There is very little that can beat it where shooting is concerned.